1

What Is Stewardship?

Stewardship is our acknowledgment that God is the Owner and Provider of all the basic goods of life, material, physical, and spiritual.

Christian stewardship is a way of life—living always as if this life were the transient thing that is in the eyes of God and His eternity. We are like young college students enrolled in a course for living in the world. We live in the dormitory and enjoy the good things that the college provides for our own lives, never losing sight of the fact that these things really belong to the college and are loaned to us. We are all stewards of the things that belong to this life!

In Deuteronomy 8:17-18, we read these words which are so applicable to our lives: "Beware lest you say in your heart, My power and the might of my hand have gotten me this wealth. You shall remember the Lord your God, for it is He who gives you power to get wealth; that He may confirm his covenant which he swore to your fathers, as this day."

Christian stewardship is not the church's method for raising money, although it is often confused in this way in the minds of people. Actually, Christian stewardship is God's way of raising Christians!

Churches that curtail their work because of a limited budget are like hospitals running half-time because there is an epidemic!

THE PRINCIPLE OF DIVINE OWNERSHIP

It is important for believers to realize that we are all stewards. The only choice we have is what kind of steward we will be.

The Word Steward

The dictionary says a steward is one who manages the estate or affairs of another. The word steward translated comes from the Greek word, *oikonomos*.

The history of this word is very interesting. It is a word which began in humility and ended in dignity. It is a word that had its beginning in filth and its conclusion in glory. The reason for a word lies not in its history, but in its sociology—not where it came from, but where it has come to be used. This word has come from the pig pen to the kingdom of God.

Sometimes in my sermons, it is important for me to remind people that everything belongs to God. The Word of God teaches us that we brought nothing into this world and it is certain we can carry nothing out.

All that we have, including our ability to accumulate material things, we receive from God above (Deuteronomy 8:18): "But thou shalt remember the Lord, thy God: for it is He that giveth power to get wealth, that He may establish His covenant which He sware unto thy fathers, as it is this day."

And it is to Him that we must someday give an account of our stewardship. Paul said, "But why doest thou judge thy brother? For we shall all stand before the judgement seat of Christ." As Christians, we must ask ourselves: What am I going to do about my responsibility to God? Am I going to be a good steward or poor steward?

To be an unfaithful steward is to miss the best in this life, and to receive the just condemnation of the great Judge of all the earth (Matthew 25:29, 30): "For unto everyone that hath shall be given, and he shall have abundance; but from him that hath not shall be taken away even that which he hath. And cast ye the unprofitable servant into outer darkness; there shall be weeping and gnashing of teeth."

But to be a good steward is to receive rewards in this life, and the commendation of his Lord in the Great Day (Matthew 25:23): "His Lord said unto him, well done, good and faithful servant; thou hast been faithful over a few things, I will make thee ruler over many things: enter thou unto the joy of thou Lord."

THE PRINCIPLE OF HUMAN STEWARDSHIP

The first questions a person must face when addressing his or her personal stewardship issues are: What shall I do with my life? Where and in what shall I invest it?

Acceptance of the principles of Jesus Christ brings the intense desire to do something about them. For example, there was that busy member of the Sanhedrin court, the highest tribunal in the life of Israel, dictating the affairs of church and state. He was zealous concerning the things he believed. He even fought those from distant lands to defend his way of life — Judaism. But in that glorious midday experience, he was knocked from his beast on the Damascus road. He received the divine question: "Saul, Saul, why persecutest thou me?" Instantaneously, he was jolted into an awareness of his possibilities as well as his responsibilities: "Lord, what will thou have me to do?"

This all came as a result of Paul seeing Christ. The whole plan of his life was changed. Who, then, was better qualified to write to the little church of Philippi than the now aged Paul? Having now passed through various changes in life (Philippians 3:4-8), he wrote: "Though I might also have confidence in the flesh. If any other man thinketh that he hath whereof he might trust in the flesh, I more.... Circumcised the eighth day of the stock of Israel of the tribe of Benjamin, Hebrew of the Hebrews; as touching the law, a Pharisee; Concerning zeal, persecuting the church; touching the righteousness which is in the law, blameless; But what things were gain to me, those I counted loss for Christ; Yea, doubtless and I count all things but loss for the excellency of the knowledge of Christ Jesus my Lord: for whom I have suffered the loss of all things and do count them but dung, that I may win Christ."

"For whether we live, we live unto the Lord: whether we die, we die unto the Lord: whether we live therefore, or die, we are the Lord's" (Romans 14:8).

Human beings are stewards in every aspect of their lives. There are many definitions for Christian stewardship, and it is important for us to remember that stewardship is the Christian law of life. It does not primarily refer to property and money, though it includes these.

"I beseech you therefore, brethren, by the mercies of God, that ye present your bodies a living sacrifice, holy, acceptable unto God, which is your reasonable service. And be not conformed to this world; but be ye transformed by the renewing of your mind, that ye may prove what is that good and acceptable and perfect will of God" (Romans 12:1-2).

Paul is pleading with each believer to give himself and his life wholly unto God. This includes the believer's all. Paul includes the body of a believer within the preview of Christian stewardship. The body is the temple of the Holy Spirit. Christians are to present their bodies unto Him, clean and holy. We are not to defile our bodies in any way. Any sinful habit which will break down the tissues, poison the system and destroy health is sinful in God's sight. This would not be "holy, acceptable to God" as Paul has said.

To be "conformed to this world" is to go the way of the world, to do the things the world does, to talk as they talk and to act as they act. Enjoying the things that the world enjoys is definitely not Christian stewardship of one's life. To be "transformed" means to be completely changed. Christians are to manifest the new life, new desires, new ambitions and new purpose in the life of a believer. This purpose is to please God. Jesus said, "If ye love me, keep my commandments." He also said, "If ye love me ye will keep my words."

The greatest evidence of a good steward is the willingness of that steward to seek to please the Master in all things. When one puts on the badge of "steward," he or she takes on a great responsibility; however, it is a good one. Christians should be happy to give themselves in service to Him who loved them and gave Himself for them.

Believers hold all they possess because they are redeemed subjects and servants of the Lord Jesus Christ. The steward owns nothing. Christ purchased and redeemed us from the bondage of sin. We are bought with a price. This is the secret of stewardship—all that one has is held as a trust for Christ. All is His. All of a Christian's possessions come under the same law. He must give all for all. God will have no divided stewardship.

The word steward or stewardship is found in the Scriptures about twenty-one times. It is used to translate several Hebrew and Greek words.

1) Abraham said, "Lord God, what wilt thou give me seeing I go childless, and the steward (son of acquisition) of my house is this Eliezer?" (Genesis 15:2).

2) And they came near to the steward (one over a household) of Joseph's house (Genesis 43:19).

3) And he commanded the steward (one over a house), of his house (Genesis 44:1).

4) Joseph said unto his steward (one over a house), up, follow after the men (Genesis 44:4).

5) He was in Titzah, drinking himself drunk in the house of Arza steward (which is over his house) in Tirzah (Kings 16:9).

6) David assembled all the princes...and the stewards (heads, chiefs, captains) over all the substance and Possessions of the king (1Chronicles 28:1).

7) The lord of the vineyard saith unto his steward (one who is committed), Call the labourers (Matthew 20:8).

8) Joanna the wife of Chuza Herod's steward (one whom a thing is committed) (Luke 8:3).

9) Who then is that faithful and wise steward (house manager), whom his lord shall make ruler over his household, to give them their portion of meat in due season (Luke 12:42).

10-16) There was a certain rich man, which had a steward (house manager); and the same was accused unto him that he had wasted his goods. And he called him, and said unto him, How is it that I hear this of thee? give an account of they stewardship (house management); for thou mayest be no longer steward (house manager). Then the steward (house manager) said within himself, what shall I do? For my lord taketh away from me the stewardship (house management); I cannot dig; to beg I am ashamed. I am resolved what to do, that when I am put out of the stewardship (house management), they may receive me into their houses ... And the lord commenced the unjust steward (house manager) (Luke 16:1-4,8).

17) Let a man so account of us, as of the ministries of Christ, and stewards (house managers) of the mysteries of God (1 Corinthians 4:1).

18) Moreover it is required in stewards (house managers), that a man be found faithful" (1 Corinthians 4:2).

19) A bishop must be blameless, as the stewards (house manager) of God (Titus 1:7).

20) As every man hath received the gift, even so minister the same one to another, as good stewards (house managers) of the manifold grace of God (1 Peter 4:10).

21) In Genesis 43:16 the word is translated "ruler" – meaning the same.

22) In Daniel 1:11 the English word "steward" is not found in the text but it is in the margin – meaning the same.

Through careful study of these words, "steward" and "stewardship," it will be seen that in every case the steward is one who handles the property or manages the affairs of another. The steward's position is one of honor, trust, and great responsibility.

2

Stewardship of Our Time

STEWARDSHIP OF TIME

There are some people who do a pretty good job of managing their money, but do just the opposite when it comes to time management. They become so involved in making a living that they don't take time to make a life. They forget that God has a right to their lives. You will so often hear people say, "I don't mind going to and giving to the church, but I just don't have the time."

The leading excuse, when I ask members about coming to prayer service and Bible class is "Pastor, I just don't have time."

When I challenge them to participate in other weekly ministries, the reply is often, "I would like to, but I just don't have time."

The "good steward" must say, "My life is a trust. "Not only does one day in seven belong to God, everyday is His. One day, we must give an account of how we handled not only our money, influence, talents, substance, and personality, but how we used our time.

Stewardship of Our Time

While time is one of our most precious gifts, it is also the most abused. Time is the wisest of counselors, the most comforting counselor, the herald of truth, the herb that cures all diseases.

> *Time is life and life is eternity*
> *Time is the bearer of good and ill, is ever near*
> *Our golden moon of harvest days, will soon be here*
> *The yellow sun is heading west*
> *Its brilliant rays on earth's soft breast*
> *Lighting the way to that long rest*
> *Whence comes no fear*
> *Time the prime minister of life will tender care*
> *Hath sheltered us where storms assailed our thoroughfare*
> *When darkness came we groped for light*
> *To shun the wrong and find the right*
> *Time to lead us onward in the fight and skies grew fair*
> *Time the keeper of life and death is almost run*
> *Our books will close with legion deeds left yet undone*
> *But comes the reaper when he may*
> *T'will not be dark along the way*
> *If thou be near on that last day.*

Arnold Bennett wrote a book entitled, *How to Live on Twenty-Four Hours a Day*. In it, he addresses the "daily miracle." You get up in the morning and lo, your purse is magically filled with twenty-four hours of manufactured tissue of the universe of your life. No one can take it away from you. No one receives either more or less than you receive. Waste it as you will and the supply will never be withheld from you. Moreover, you cannot draw on the future. It is impossible to go into time debt. You can only waste the passing moments. You cannot waste tomorrow, it is kept for you. What you do with your twenty-four hours a day will determine the attitude of your stewardship. You have the management as a steward over 168 hours each week. What are your going to do with them?

In the proper use of time, one might care to use the suggested outline:

Planning Your Time

1. Sleep
2. Work
3. Recreation
   A. play – amusements
   B. physical exercise
   C. clubs, societies, etc.
4. Self-Improvement
   A. reading – study – lectures
   B. music
   C. art
5. Family and Social Intercourse (including meals)
6. Worship and Religious Cultivation
   A. public service and worship
   B. private Bible reading
   C. private prayer
7. Service
   A. religious (church work)
   B. community (social work)
   C. politics

This is a suggested time outline for those who wish to be better stewards of time.

Steward of Our Time Lesson

Objective: To become wise stewards of all that God has created us to be individually.

Stewardship of Our Time

Memory Verse: Galatians 2:20
Read: Romans 12
Bible Study—Read: Psalm 90:12
Question: What should be our prayer concerning the use of time that God gives us?

A. Right Attitude About Time

1. What do good stewards do? (Ephesians 5:16)

2. Why is proper use of our time so important today? (James 4:14)

3. What does God demand of us concerning the stewardship of our time? (Psalm 62:8)

4. What does Christ admonish us to do as stewards of time until He comes again? (Mark 13:33-37)

5. If we are wise stewards and heed the commands of our Master, how will we use our time? (Ephesians 5:15, 16)

B. Right Relationship with God

1. As wise stewards concerned over the use of our time, what will we want to understand? (Ephesians 5:17)

2. What is necessary in order to fully know the will of God concerning our stewardship duties? (Ephesians 5:18)

3. The Holy Spirit will enable the faithful steward to perform the duties of stewardship by giving what to the steward? (Acts 1:8)

4. He will perform these duties in the name of whom? (Colossians 3:17)

5. What then, will be our attitude as we utilize the time over which God has made us stewards? (Ephesians 5:19, 20)

6. How would you describe such a useful and joyous life? (John 10:10b)

C. Most Important Use of Time

1. As wise stewards who know and are obedient to the will of God, we can be sure we will spend much of our time doing what? (Mark 16:15)

2. What does God say about a soul winner? (Proverb 11:30)

3. Of what value is only one soul, according to Christ?

4. What then is the greatest thing believers can do for one another?

5. What happens in God's presence when one repents and receives Christ? (Luke 15:7, 10)

6. How did Paul feel about those whom he had won to Christ? (1 Thessalonians 2:19, 20)

LIFE APPLICATION QUESTIONS

1. How many hours are there in a week?

2. Why is it that some may accomplish more than others in the same amount of time?

3

Stewardship of Our Bodies

Paul had heard of the church at Rome, but he had never been there, nor had any of the other apostles. Evidently, the church was begun by Jews who had come to faith during Pentecost (Acts 2). "They spread the faith on their return to Rome and the church grew."

Although many barriers separated them, Paul felt a bond with these Romans. They were his brothers and sisters in Christ, and he longed to see them face to face. He had never met most of the Christians in Rome, yet he loved them. He sent a letter to introduce himself and to make a clear declaration of the faith. In it, he talks about the freedom that comes from being saved —freedom from the power of sin (6:1-23); freedom from the domination of the Law (7:1-25); freedom to become like Christ and discover God's limitless love.

In Romans 12:1-2, he writes to them and to us today: And so, dear brothers, I plead with you to give your bodies to God. Let them be a living sacrifice, holy —the kind He can accept. When you think of what He has done for you, is this too much to ask? Don't copy the behavior and customs of this world, but be a new and different person with a newness in all you do and think. Then you will learn from your own experience how His ways will really satisfy you.

Paul is saying that God wants us to offer ourselves, not animals, as living sacrifices—daily laying aside our own desires to follow Him. We do this out of gratitude that our sins have been forgiven.

He says that God has good, pleasing and perfect plans for His children. He wants us to be new people with freshness of thought, alive to glorify Him. Since He wants only what is best for us, and since He gave His Son to make our new lives possible, we should joyfully offer ourselves as living sacrifices to Him.

STEWARDSHIP OF OUR BODIES LESSON

Objective: To surrender our bodies to Christ from the heart.
Memory Verse: Psalm 139:23-24
Read: Psalm 51; Galatians 5; Ephesians 5
Bible Study Read: Hebrews 10:1-10.

A. The Spirit and the Body

1. Every person is to be renewed in the spirit of his or her mind if that person is to be converted to Christ. How was that conversion made possible? (Hebrews 10:1-10)

2. What do you learn about the body of the Christian from Romans 8:8-9 and Romans 12:1?

3. Express, in your own words, the additional reasons given in 1 Corinthians 6:19-20 for being a good steward of your body.

◦○ Stewardship of Our Bodies ○◦

B. The Parts of the Body

1. The Tongue

   a) Why is it so important to be a good steward of the tongue? (James 3:2-6) What should you know concerning its use? (Matthew 12:36)

2. The Heart

   a) What must we understand about the heart? (Jeremiah 17:9)

   b) Therefore, what should a steward of God continually pray? (Psalm 139:23, 24)

   c) What should be done about sin? (1 John 1:9)

   d) What condition of the heart does God require? (Psalm 51:17)

   e) What kind of heart does God look for and why? (2 Chronicles 16:9)

3. The Mind

   a) What is your responsibility to being a steward of your mind? (1 Peter 1:13)

   b) Whose mind and which qualities thereof should you have? (Philippians 2:5-8; 1 Corinthians 2:12-16)

   c) What is the result of keeping your mind stayed on the Lord? (Isaiah 26:3)

   d) How can you keep your mind on Him? (Philippians 4:6, 7; (Proverbs 4:20-22)

C. Sexual Expression

1. What do the sins spoken against in 1 Corinthians 6:9-10; 13-18, mainly involve?

≈ What in the World Is Christian Stewardship? ≈

2. God considered David a man after His own heart, yet David's great sin was what? (2 Samuel 11:14-15; 26-27)

3. What is God's stern judgment against misusers and abusers of sex? (1 Corinthians 6:9-11)

4. Why is it especially tragic if a Christian becomes involved in the misuse of sex? (1 Corinthians 6:15-18)

5. How serious is sexual lust, according to Christ? (Matthew 5:28)

6. How can the application of the following verses enable one to overcome sexual lust? (Philippians 4:8; Psalm 119:11; 1 Corinthians 10:13; Romans 6:14)

LIFE APPLICATION

1. How can the stewardship of each part of the body affect the other parts? How can stewardship of each part affect the body as a whole?

2. How would you apply 1 Thessalonians 5:22 to:

   a) The use of the tongue?

   b) The desires of your heart?

   c) The control of your mind?

   d) Your conduct with members of the opposite sex?

4

Stewardship of Our Gifts

STEWARDSHIP OF OUR TALENTS AND GIFTS

Life's resources and powers, whether great or small, many or few, inherent or acquired, are all to be managed on the basis of Christian stewardship. We are but trustees of these things and are accountable to God for the way in which we use them or misuse them.

There are those who are blessed with more talents than others. Some have five, some have two and still others have but one. All believers do not have the same number nor degree of talents, but all believers have equal responsibility to use any and all talents with the same degree of faithfulness.

Some people, well aware of their abilities, believe they have the right to use them as they please. Others feel they have no special talent at all. Everyone has some ability. If you don't know what yours are, find out and use them to the glory of God. All of our abilities should be dedicated in Christian service to others, none are for our own exclusive enjoyment.

In 1 Corinthians 12, Paul writes and teaches about spiritual gifts. The special abilities given to each person by the Holy Spirit are called spiritual gifts. They enable us to minister to the needs of the body of believers. There are many gifts. People have different gifts, and no gift is superior to another. All gifts come from the Holy Spirit, and their purpose is to build up Christ's body, the Church.

Instead of building and unifying the Corinthian church, spiritual gifts were splitting them into factions. Spiritual gifts had become symbols of spiritual power, causing rivalries and establishing hierarchies of supposed spiritual and unspiritual people. This was a terrible misuse of spiritual gifts, because their purpose is always to help the church function more effectively, not to divide it.

The Church is comprised of many types of people from a variety of backgrounds, and possessing a multitude of gifts and abilities. Despite their differences, however, all believers have one thing in common—faith in Christ.

STEWARDSHIP OF OUR GIFTS LESSON

Introduction/Objective: To recognize our talents and abilities and to surrender them to God for His use and glory.

Memory Verse: 1 Peter 4:10

Read: 1 Corinthians 12

God created humankind with a great variety of talents. The Christian Church is comprised of people endowed with different gifts and abilities. All that the Christian possesses should be dedicated fully to God to be used as He directs.

The lesson scripture refers to the Church as the Body of Christ. Christ is its Head (1 Corinthians 12:27; Ephesians 5:23). Just as your body has many specialized parts, each having its own function, so the Church is comprised of many individuals, each having a special function to perform, and a contribution to make to the rest of the body.

Every Christian possesses both natural and spiritual gifts (abilities and talents). For they come to us at physical birth. Spiritual gifts are special abilities imparted by the Holy Spirit to Christians. These enable Christians to minister to others on behalf of Christ.

SPIRITUAL GIFTS BIBLE STUDY

A. Natural Gifts

1. What talents and natural abilities do you possess?
2. How did you acquire them?
3. According to 1 Corinthians 4:6-7 what should your attitude be about natural gifts?
4. How would you apply Colossians 3:17 to the stewardship of your natural gifts?

B. Spiritual Gifts

1. Major passages on spiritual gifts found in the Bible are: Romans 12:3-8; 1 Corinthians 12:1-31; Ephesians 4:4-16; and 1 Peter 4:10-11. From these passages, make a composite list of these spiritual gifts (combine any two that might be identical). After each gift you list, give a brief definition of that gift. (You may wish to consult a concordance or a Bible dictionary).

Spiritual Gift	Definitions
_____	_____
_____	_____
_____	_____

2. List any other spiritual gifts you can think of that might be included. Why do you think so?

3. What are some reasons God has given gifted persons to the church? (1 Corinthians 12:4-6)

4. Why will two people not exercise the same gift in the same manner? (1 Corinthians 12:4-6)

5. Though some spiritual gifts seem to be of greater value than others (1 Corinthians 12:28-31), what ideas does Paul stress keeping Christians from personal pride because of the gifts they possess? (Romans 12:4, 5; 1 Corinthians 12:12-26; 1 Corinthians 13; Ephesians 4:11-16)

6. List the principles concerning what your attitude and responsibilities are to be toward your spiritual gifts. (Romans 12:3-8)

LIFE APPLICATION

Realize that you have at least one spiritual gift, and probably more (1 Corinthians 12:11).

To find out what your spiritual gifts are, pray that God will make them known to you. Determine which of your activities the Lord seems to bless and inquire of other mature Christians who likely know well what your spiritual gifts might be. Make a list of what you believe may be your spiritual gifts.

Seek to develop your gifts in the power of the Holy Spirit, according to the scriptural exhortations. Realize that you may have other gifts of which you are not personally aware, so exercise various gifts.

Take spiritual responsibility. Be aware that you are accountable to God for stewardship of your spiritual gifts.

5

Stewardship of Our Possessions

While it is essential for us to be good stewards of our personalities, talents, time, gifts, etc., it is also important for us to be good managers of our money. A person cannot separate his or her money from his or her life, nor deal with it on a different plane. One's money cannot be spent in a way that is opposite from what one does with his or her life. If one is a good steward in other areas of life, that one must necessarily be a faithful steward of personal possessions. Personality and possessions cannot be divorced. A person cannot be a true steward of the one and not the other.

Our stewardship begins, not in our giving, but in our getting. It includes all that is involved in the acquisition of our possessions. It includes, as well, a stewardship of administration over all that is acquired. Stewardship is trusteeship, not ownership, and that involves administration. R.T. Danielson has said, "A man has no more right to determine the terms and conditions of his stewardship than he has to determine the terms of admission into the kingdom of God." This prerogative belongs to God, and in His Holy Word, He has set them forth. For every person who deliberately denies God's vested property rights in all things, there are a host of others who proudly accede to this principle verbally, yet deny it in practice. In their prayers, their worship, their hymns, these persons affirm:

> *"All that we have is Thine alone
> A trust O' Lord from Thee."*

In their actual living, however, these same persons use their possessions as if those things belonged to them, and as if they could use what they have as they please. They have no sense of trusteeship, and make no acknowledgement of their stewardship. For it is God that not only gives us power to obtain wealth, but rules in the earthly kingdom, as He told Nebuchadnezzar (Daniel 2:1-46): "He setteth up whom He will and taketh down whom He pleases." The "Good Steward" must be ever mindful that he or she is only a steward and that God is the Owner.

STEWARDSHIP OF OUR POSSESSIONS LESSON

Objective: To surrender all our material wealth to God and to Give in joy and gratitude.

Memory Verses: Luke 16:13

Read: 2 Corinthians 9; Matthew 6:19-34; 25:14-30; Luke 12:15-21

Bible Study:

A. Money—The Old Standard
1. What did God command those under the Law of Moses to do? (Malachi 3:8-10)
2. What would you say the "storehouse" is? (Deuteronomy 16:11,12; 5:5, 6)

Stewardship of Our Possessions

3. How much is a tithe? (Hebrews 7:2)

B. Money—The New Standard

1. As believers in Christ, we are under grace, rather than Law. Whereas the Law in itself did not provide eternal life for those who attempted to keep it (Galatians 2:16; 3:21-22), we have received life by the favor of God, though we do not deserve it and could not possibly earn it. Therefore, do we have a higher or lower motivation and standard for stewardship of our possessions than those under the Law?

2. How did Jesus regard a person's responsibility in this area? (Matthew 23:33)

3. In 2 Corinthians 8-9, Paul attempts to encourage the Corinthian church to give financially to help the needy Christians. He first pointed them to the example of the Macedonian church. What did the Macedonians do before they gave their money to God? (2 Corinthians 8:5)

   a) In light of this, what do you think God is most interested in?

   b) Therefore, why is giving money an important part of our Christian life, according to 2 Corinthians 8:7?

   c) Who is the great example of giving? (2 Corinthians 8:9)

   d) In what sense does one who "sows" (or gives) sparingly reap sparingly? (2 Corinthians 9:6)

   e) What kind of giver does God love? (2 Corinthians 9:7)

C. Other Possessions

1. To whom do you and your possessions belong? (1 Corinthians 6:19, 20)

2. What should be your motive in the use of whatever you possess? (1 Corinthians 10:31)

LIFE APPLICATION

1. Consider your income and possessions. What should you keep for yourself as God's steward?

3. Ask yourself, "Is my heart's attitude one of joy and gratefulness as I give?"

RECAP

1. Define the meaning of "Christian stewardship" in your own words.

2. Why are we referred to as Christian stewards?

3. Summarize your responsibilities as a steward of God as you now understand them.

4. List several things over which you exercise that stewardship.

5. What is the most important thing for you to realize about your attitude toward stewardship?

6. In what particular area of your life have you seen improvement in your Christian stewardship?

6

Giving in the Early Church

When we use the term "early church," we think about the Church as it is empowered in the Book of Acts. There we can see how the early church grew through the witness of believers "both in Jerusalem" and in "all Judea" and in "Samaria" and unto the uttermost parts of the world. (Acts 1:8) As Luke continues, he shows us how the church in Jerusalem was persecuted, and how believers were forced to scatter throughout the whole world. (Acts 8:1). He shows how the church moved out from Jerusalem, and in less than thirty-five years, captured the very capital of the world, Rome itself.

An examination of several passages and stories in Acts will reveal how they gave in the early church. Verses 44-45 of chapter two tell us something about the spirit of giving in the early church. These verses portray the spirit of the believers in the early church and their attitude toward possessions. It talks about their willingness to help one another. Some of them sold their property, houses, and other valuables and gave the money to their brethren "as every man had need."

They were under no obligation or divine command to do this.

PETER AND JOHN ENCOUNTER A BEGGAR

Acts 3 provides us with another view of how they gave in the early church. The setting was the hour of prayer and Peter and John were on their way into the Temple to pray. As they approached the Temple, their eyes fell upon a blind man who was begging at the gate. He was poor, lame, and crippled from birth. He was not able to work for a living, so he lived on alms that he received at the gate called Beautiful, believed to be one of the busiest entrances to the Temple. The man asked Peter and John for money. That was the most he expected from them and others who entered the Temple. He never thought about walking, just money. Silver and gold were all that was on his mind.

We must never allow Satan to lead us to believe that silver and gold will solve all of our problems. Many people have money and all of the things it can buy, yet their children still rebel and give them problems. Disease and tragedy do not run away from those who have money. Time does not back up one second for the wealthy. The rich man who refused to share with Lazarus found out too late that money will not do everything (Luke 16:19-31). With all that he possessed, he was still tormented in hell. The rich farmer who decided to be selfish found out that money will not delay death (Luke 12:16-21). The rich young ruler found out that money would not buy him eternal life (Matthew 19:16-21).

The man who sat at the gate begged for silver and gold, but even after years of begging, he was still a helpless, hopeless, crippled man. No amount of money could strengthen his joints and allow him to walk.

∽ Giving In The Early Church ∾

Anybody could give him money but Peter and John offered him something better. Believers must stand up in the midst of this capitalistic, greedy society we live in and remind people that money will not do everything. Peter and John offered him something better. Peter looked on this man with eyes of compassion. He watched how Jesus had compassion on people. He knew of the story of the good Samaritan, they saw him heal the sick, and raise the dead. Through their association with Jesus, the two had absorbed His spirit and were now demonstrating that spirit.

Peter and John, through their example, left us with three simple rules of Christian sharing.

THEY SHARED WHAT THEY HAD

Someone has said, "Never let what you cannot do stop you from doing what you can for God." We may not have an abundance of everything, but we must be willing to share what we have. Peter and John could have walked away because they didn't have silver or gold, but they were willing to share what they had. How poor they appeared and yet they were so rich! They lived by faith, carrying no purse as they went about preaching. Their visible resources were zero, but their invisible resources were unlimited. Sometimes we look around and see others who have so much that we feel sorry for ourselves. But if we are in relationship with God, we have unlimited resources.

THEY GAVE WHAT THEY HAD
IN JESUS' NAME

Oh that name, Jesus! It is in that name that we find the merit of our gifts. The merit of our gifts has very little to do with us; it is His name. In the name of Jesus lies the power of the giver. If you think you do not have a lot to offer, just give what you do have in His name. A little given in Jesus' name will go a long, long way. Just ask the lad who had only the makings of a fish sandwich, but turned it over to Jesus, who blessed it and fed thousands (John 6:9). Yes, there is power in that name which to every knee must bow, and every tongue must confess. Acts 4:12 says, "neither is there salvation in any other; for there is none other name under heaven given among men, whereby, we must be saved."

Everything we do, every act of praise and worship, every gift we give, ought to be given in His name. We must be careful not to do things for people for selfish reasons.

They Gave Something Better Than Silver and Gold

Silver and gold are quickly spent. Our health fails, sooner or later. The undertaker always wins over the doctor. Only that which is done for the soul is eternal. To give silver and gold without giving Jesus is to leave another poor indeed. We, like Peter and John, may not have silver and gold, but we must give what we have. We may not have all the riches of this world, but we must be willing to share what we have in the name of Jesus. Silver and gold cannot make a house into a home. It will not make fathers stay home and take care of their families. Silver and gold will not stop people from hating each other. Silver and gold will not solve our racial problems. Silver and gold will not solve the dropout problem and the drug problem that robs so many young people of a future. Silver and gold have their place, but only Christ will make a real difference in our world. We must give people Jesus, even though they may be begging for other things.

As the story ends, we see the results of their giving. The man was able to walk because of the miraculous healing power of Jesus. The man did his part and Peter did his, but it was the power in the name of Jesus that put strength in his limbs. He leaped up, and walked into the Temple to praise God. As we continue to read this book in Chapter 4, we find the believers sharing their possessions: "and the multitude of them that ought of the things which he possessed was his own; but they had all things common and with great power gave the apostles witness of the resurrecting of the Lord Jesus; and great grace was upon them all. Neither was there any among them that lacked; for as many as were possessors of lands or houses sold them, and brought the process of the things that were sold. And laid them down at the apostles feet: and distributions man according as he had" (vv. 33-35).

How easy it would be to solve the world's hunger and housing problems if those who have an abundance had the proper attitude about what God had entrusted to them. If we really lived like everything we have belongs to God, we could take care of our poor and needy. Verse 36: "And Jesus, who by the apostles was surnamed Barnabas, which is being interpreted, the son of consolation, a Levite, and of the country of Cyprus." Verse 37: "Having land, sold it and brought the money, and laid it at the apostle's feet."

The record states that Barnabas sold the land he owned. As a Levite, he knew that he had the Lord God of Israel for his inheritance. As one who would deliver the Good News of the Gospel, Barnabas disentangled himself from the affairs of this life. He lost nothing by laying the money at the apostles' feet, although he was, in effect, numbered among the apostles, by the Word of the Holy Ghost.

This act would be viewed by many in our society and in our churches as unthinkable because we allow our possessions to own and control us, instead of us owning and controlling them. Just think of the financial blessings our churches would experience if people would give according to the leading of the Holy Spirit. While we pray about many things, I wonder if we sincerely pray and talk to God about our giving. Our churches suffer and many times are unable to do the work of the church because we do not have enough money to operate.

ANANIAS AND SAPPHIRA

The next story of early church stewardship illustrates how we can mess up when we face the Spirit and we take our giving into our hands. Acts 5 tells of a man named Ananias who, along with his wife Sapphira, sold a possession. It appears here that a trend was beginning in the early church, though not everyone was sincere and honest in their giving to the Lord's church.

There are a lot of Ananias' and Sapphira's in our churches, people who try to do what others are doing, but with selfish motives. We must be aware of the fact that God is not just interested in the amount we give, but also in our attitudes about what we give. Second Corinthians 9:7 it tells us: "Every man according as he purposeth in his heart, so let him give; not grudgingly, or of necessity; for God loveth a cheerful giver."

When we give, it should be done with much thought and design, not by accident. The problem here is that the couple sold the land, but kept a portion of the money from the sale. Keep in mind that this business of selling possessions was not commanded of them by Scripture but was something that their hearts lead them to do. When we make pledges to the church, we should keep in mind that it's dangerous to pledge and promise to do things for God and then fail to follow through. We should not do things just because someone else is doing something. Our giving should be a response to God's Word and our gratitude for all of His blessings toward us.

What Was Their Sin?

The problem with Ananias and Sapphira was not that they kept part of the money, but that they lied about keeping the money. They had vowed to give the money to the church, but kept back part of the proceeds instead. They only laid part of the money at the feet of the apostles. Obviously, this was a well-thought-out plan to deceive the church. It is clear from verse 2 that Ananias and Sapphira were a part of a scheme — they appeared to be sincere about their gift, but they tried to mock God, and deceive others. They wanted credit for being disciples, but they would not make the sacrifice, and so they were a discredit to discipleship. They coveted worldly wealth, and were mistrustful of God and His providence.

Ananias and Sapphira thought they could get away with their scheme. The same Holy Spirit that empowers us and directs us in righteousness, will also reveal our sins and shortcomings. This is not done to hurt us, but to help us.

Peter apparently saw through their scheme, by the power given to him by the Holy Spirit. He detected their deception and controlled them. They lacked the faith to believe that God could take care of them, so they tried to provide for themselves. Are we that way? Busy trying to be our own security? Make our own way when we have a loving, caring, responsible, resourceful Father who knows all of our needs and will supply them? Ephesians 3:20 tells us "Now unto him that is able to do exceeding abundantly above all that we ask or think, according to the power that worketh in us."

Ananias' and Sapphira's sin was that they came with a great show of piety and laid the money at the apostles' feet as though they had given their all. Peter reminded them that it was never mandatory to sell their land, nor was it necessary to give the money, even after they sold the land. They had the power to do the right thing, but didn't. Acts like this led some to believe that money is the root of all evil, but that's not what the Scripture teaches. It tells us in 1 Timothy 6:10, "for the *love of* money is the root of all evil; which while some coveted after, they have earned from the faith, and pierced themselves through with many sorrows."

THEY LIED AND DIED

Peter informed Ananias that he lied to the Holy Spirit — a sin of a heinous nature, and how he could not have been guilty of it if Satan had not filled his heart. Don't ever forget that Satan is a lying spirit. Peter said that Ananias did not lie to man, but to God. Those who lied to the apostles are said to have lied to God, because the apostles acted by the power and authority of God.

What happens when we lie to the Spirit? In the case of Ananias, he fell down and died. He was speechless, as we are when caught lying. Not only was he speechless, but he died at the very spot where he lied! There are various opinions about this. Some believe an angel struck him, or perhaps the horror and amazement at his guilt caused him to fall under the load of it. Others say he fell when he remembered the unpardonable state of a blasphemer against the Holy Spirit, it struck him like a dagger to his heart.

I wonder what the effect would be today if everyone who has ever lied about what they give to the church would drop dead! Have you ever lied about something that you promised to give to God or do for Him? Have you ever raised your hand for a pledge and then refused to be faithful to that pledge? If you have, then you should be praising God for His mercy. Like Ananias and Sapphira, great fear should come upon us when we realize what God could do to us, but instead He extends mercy.

The young men carried Ananias out and buried him immediately, as was the custom of the Jews. Unfortunately, this story of selfish giving does not end with the death of Ananias. His wife, Sapphira, met the same consequences. Verse 7 says about three hours after the burial of her husband, Sapphira, not knowing what had happened, came in. Peter gave her a chance to make this situation right by asking her, "Was this all you received for the sale of the land, and had you no more for it?" But she, like her husband, lied.

It said that our lies and deception cause other people to lie and be deceptive. The couple agreed to tell the same story. No one could disprove them; therefore they thought they might safely stand in the lie. Peter was fair, however. Before he passed sentence, he made her know her sins, and showed her the evil of it. Sentence was carried out, and since she lied like her husband, she paid the same price. She fell dead at Peter's feet. The men carried her out and buried her beside her husband.

Adam and Eve were driven from the Garden of Eden because of sin. Likewise, Ananias and Sapphira were driven from the world through death because of their sin. Great fear came upon the church and everyone who witnessed this tragedy. It certainly should have taught them and us a lesson about trying to deceive God! It should also teach us to be very serious about our commitment to God's will and God's work.

Good Stewards of Our Time

Acts 6 gives us a story about giving; not money, but the giving of ourselves and establishing our priorities as servants of God. Part of the ministry of the Church is to care for those who cannot care for themselves. As the church grew, so did the need for help with its many ministries. The number of disciples was multiplied and there arose a murmuring, the Grecians begin to complain about being neglected in the daily distribution of food. They alleged that the Hebrew widows were better cared for than them.

When I read this passage, I always think about how we argue sometimes about food in the church. Not only that, but how one group becomes jealous of another, thus hindering the spiritual progress of the church. What was the answer to this dilemma? The apostles were already giving themselves to preaching the gospel, but they recognized the need to settle this situation. The twelve assembled the people and explained that it was not reasonable for them to quit preaching the gospel to serve tables. The apostles instructed them to find seven men of honest report who could be trusted — men full of the Holy Spirit and wisdom — and they would appoint them over this ministry.

As we study this situation, we come to understand that this ministry involved more than just distributing food. Duties such as receiving and paying of money needed trustworthy servants just like those serving tables. Today we call these helpers deacons, or stewards. They were appointed to take care of that ministry. They couldn't just be any kind of people; they had to be fully qualified, trustworthy, wise, and full of the Holy Spirit.

The apostles realized that it was more important for them to be unhindered in preaching the gospel, and to give themselves continually to prayer, and the ministry of the Word. Many of our churches today have a tremendous amount of what I call "soul ministries" (such as food ministries, self-help programs, etc.). While all of these social ministries are good, they must not overshadow the most important ministry — preaching God's Word. We must always be about the business of advancing the kingdom of God.

Who Did They Choose?

The apostles chose Stephen, a man full of faith and of the Holy Spirit, and Philip, Prochorus, Nicanor, and Timon, Parmenas, and Nicolas a proselyte of Antioch. They set these men before the apostles and prayed and they laid their hands on them. The Scriptures tell us that the Word of God increased and the number of the disciples multiplied in Jerusalem greatly; and a great company of the priests were obedient to the faith.

God's kingdom will always advance when we determine that the preaching of God's Word is our number one priority. Those of us who love the Lord must establish our priorities, then we must be willing to give our time, money, and talent to the glory of God. If we would do that, in times like we live, we could truly make a difference in our churches, our homes, our communities, and even our world.

7

Stop Throwing Your Money Away!

BUY LIFE INSURANCE ONLINE

Mix fear of death with a distaste for salesmen, and you can see why many people procrastinate about buying life insurance. As a licensed insurance broker for 24 years, I've had many experiences with those who never get around to buying life insurance as well a those who don't buy enough of it. Well, your computer cannot keep death from visiting you, but it can free you from having to rely on outdated rules of thumb. (Your coverage should equal seven times your income.) You can save up to 40 percent on annual premiums when you shop for policies online.

Here's a rundown on the three main ways you can use your computer to become a wiser life insurance shopper.

Over the past few years, several web sites and software packages have provided access to sophisticated calculations – essentially electronic worksheets – that let you determine the amount of insurance your family would need to replace your income or your spouse's should one of you die. You spend about 15 minutes online typing in such information as your age, annual income, the size of your investment portfolio and your living expenses. Once you are done, the estimation instantly displays the amount of insurance you need.

Other calculations – such as those included in software packages like Managing Your Money® – can perform the same basic calculation. But they tend to make some inflexible assumptions — for example, that all your assets will be sold after your death to generate income for your family. Quick Quote®, on the other hand, asks if you want to exclude from the analysis assets such as investments earmarked for your spouse's retirement.

CHOOSING THE RIGHT TYPE OF POLICY

Plenty of sites purport to outline the pros and cons of the confusing array of life insurance policies being peddled these days. Some offer cash-value insurance (those that combine insurance with a savings account and generate the juiciest commissions). Others offer term insurance which offers basic insurance protection at an initial cost of as much as 85 percent below that of cash-value policies. When it comes to shopping online, you are pretty much limited to term policies. With only a few exceptions, the vast majority of people are better off with term insurance. To get a price quote online, you enter such information as your date of birth, the amount of coverage you desire, and the length of time you wish to lock-in the policy's premium. If you decide to buy, you can fill in an application online.

Tips on How to Spend Less on your Home and Car Insurance and More

– Home –

Home – Relocate to a Cheaper Area – You may be earning a higher income in a certain area or region of the country, but how much more is it costing you to live? Consider relocation to an area or region that offers a lower cost of living.

Refinance Your Mortgage – If you can get an interest rate that is even one percent lower than your current mortgage rate, and you plan to stay in your house long enough to recoup the up-front costs (generally two to four percent of the mortgage interest amount), refinancing is probably an option for you to consider. Because most Americans stay in their homes an average of six years, think about trading in your conventional fixed rate loan for a Hybrid Adjustable Rate Mortgage (ARM). Your savings can be significant.

Consider a hypothetical scenario: A couple takes a 30-year fixed mortgage at 9.03 percent in 1984, with monthly payments of $807. Had they refinanced to a seven-one ARM at a rate of 7.4 percent (that means the interest is locked in for seven years and then is adjusted annually) their monthly payment would have dropped sixteen percent, to $682 per month. During the next seven years they would save twenty percent, or $12,356.

Lower Your Energy Bills – When you have to replace your furnace or air conditioner, consider a geothermal heat pump instead. During winter, these underground systems pull heat from the earth and pump it into the house. In summer, they pull heat out of the house. A geothermal system generally $3,000 to

$5,000 more than traditional heating and cooling system. Monthly utility savings of 20 to 70 percent will result—meaning you usually recoup your investment in three to five years.

Challenge Your Property Tax Assessment – An estimated one-third of all U.S. homes are assessed at a higher value than they are worth. Tax experts say that more than half of the people who challenge their assessment win a tax reduction averaging ten percent.

AUTOMOBILES/TRANSPORTATION

Purchase a Used Car — A new car typically achieves half of its five-year depreciation during the first two years of ownership. By letting someone else own the car during the first two years, you will not only pay significantly less than the new car sticker price, you will also get more for your money, according to Charles Donaldson, director of research at the Campbell, California research firm, IntelliChoice.

Considering a Car Buying Service — Having someone else to negotiate the purchase price of your vehicle can save you ten percent or more off the average new car costing $21,480. You could spend your weekends pounding car lots and haggling to cut a dealer's profit margin, but why not save your soles by signing up with a professional car buying service?

For a fee of $250 to $500, your proxy will seek out the best price on the auto you want from competing dealers and will close the deal for you.

Choose a Car that is Cheap to Own Over a Car that is Cheap to Buy — Over five years or so, the cost to maintain a car is more expensive than its purchase price, according to IntelliChoice President Levy.

Fine-Tune Your Car Insurance — Experts advise that one of the simplest ways to cut car insurance premiums is to increase the deductible amount.

Meals/Entertainment

Buy in Bulk — For an average of $25 a year you can join a wholesale warehouse club which sells groceries, auto supplies, electronics and more at prices that are often 25 percent less than at traditional retail outlets. You might also join a food coop. These groups are usually listed in the Yellow Pages® under "food plans," "food services" or "health stores." Buy bulk quantities of groceries such as meat, fish, pasta and vegetables.

Use Discount Dining Cards — Discount dining cards have grown in acceptance as more upscale restaurants have agreed to participate. Every card has its own rules and selection of eating establishments, but all work on roughly the same principle. Normally, there is an annual fee of $25 to $50 and the plan qualifies the cardholder for meal discounts or rebates of 10 to 25 percent.

Affordable Vacations — Travel when others don't. You can save 25 to 50 percent of vacation costs if you travel during the off season. For example, cruise lovers can often save 25 percent or more by sailing to places such as the Caribbean in fall instead of winter.

Save on Airline Tickets — As much as 60 percent or more can be cut off full-fare prices if tickets are purchased at least twenty-one days in advance of your trip. If you can't manage that, then try a travel consolidation, which buys blocks of unused tickets from airlines and resells them to travelers at discounts of up to 50 percent. As a rule, consolidation offers the best savings on last-minute overseas trips.

Save on Hotel Rooms — Similar to airline consolidation, hotel discounters buy blocks of rooms from major chains and resells them to consumers at discounts of twenty-five to sixty-five percent.

Join Travel Discount Programs — You will pay annual dues of $25 to $100 to join one of these organizations which offers discounts of 25 to 50 percent on hotels, rental cars, and sometimes, air fares.

CLOTHING

Hunt for Bargains — You may have to push through crowds and avant garde orange suits, but savings of as much as 75 percent justify regular visits to off-price department stores. Their aisles are filled with last year's styles, buyouts and this year's overstock. Such stores generally feature high-quality, name brand merchandise at a price lower than normal retail. Caution: avoid "impulse" purchases! Even at a bargain price, such purchases are costly in the long run.

Do Not Forget to Haggle — I'm not suggesting that you shop as though you are in a Middle East bazaar. But there's no reason you can't request, say, free alterations when buying an expensive suit or dress. Similarly, if you pay full price for an item that is marked down soon after your purchase, request an adjustment in your purchase price. Most stores have this as an unadvertised policy.

HEALTH CARE COSTS

Investigate Managed Health Care – Your monthly premiums may be higher than with traditional fee-for-service insurance, but your total out of pocket costs could drop by more than 20 percent. Reason: managed care plans generally do not require a deductible and the fees for office visits are generally zero to $15. Both differences are crucial for families that generally have multiple yearly visits to the doctor for common childhood ailments. For example, there are two basic types of plans: health maintenance organizations (HMOs), which can restrict your choice of doctors, and preferred provider organizations (PPOs), which allow you choose from doctors outside the plan. Your employer may offer both. See your employer's health plan administrator for more information.

If You Have a Fee-for-Service Insurance Plan, Raise Your Deductible – As with car and homeowner's insurance, if you cover the small stuff yourself, you can cut your health insurance premiums. By raising a $1000 deductible to $1500, the average family of four could reduce their premiums by 26 percent.

Reduce Prescription Costs – Ask your doctor if there is a generic alternative to your prescription. If so, you can typically cut prescription bills by 60 percent or more. In addition, mail-order pharmacies can cut your pharmaceutical costs by as much as 75 percent on some prescriptions, providing you can plan ahead and wait two weeks or so for delivery.

Try An "Urgent Care" Clinic – These facilities generally charge 25 percent to 75 percent less than a visit to your doctor or a hospital emergency room. They are ideal for treating non-life threatening injuries such as a broken bone, a scrape, or the flu. Check your Yellow Pages® for a clinic near you.

Your Children's Education

Search for the Best College Values – The average cost for four years of tuition, fees, housing and meals is considerably less at a public college than a private college. Before you scoff at the idea of sending your child to a state school instead of an Ivy League school, know that many state schools offer comparable or superior education.

Put Your Children on a Fast Track – More than 300 colleges allow students to pursue graduate degrees while completing their bachelor's degree course work in three years. Alternatively, more than 1000 schools allow students to schedule extra courses during the academic year, while granting credit for basic courses completed during the summer at cheaper schools back home or for advanced placement courses completed in high school. Both strategies require a lot of effort, but the savings may be worth the sweat. Reference books to help you learn more about these options are available at most bookstores and libraries). Some contain a list of schools with combined degree and accelerated programs.

Scoop up Scholarships – An estimated 1.25 billion in scholarships is awarded each year to some 750,000 students. Over twice that amount goes unclaimed each year. You can find a lot of information out about scholarship and grants on the Internet through the Fin-Aid web site (www.finaid.org), a service which offers links to over forty scholarship databases.

YOUR FINANCES

Cut Your Plastic Payments in Half—The typical U.S. family owns 14 credit cards with an average total balance of $5,800. At an average 17 percent annual interest, that comes to $986 a year in finance charges. There is no reason to pay that much when nearly 20 U.S. banks offer cards with interest rates of 10 percent or less. Switching to such a card could save a family almost $500 a year or more.

Consolidate Your Debt into a Home Equity Loan—Paying off your high-rate credit card balances with a home equity loan has two advantages. First, the average home equity loan interest rate is much lower (recently 9.6 percent). Second, the home equity interest on borrowing up to $100,000 is tax deductible.

Take Advantage of Rebate Cards—Although rules for rebate deals are tightening, they are worth a look. For every dollar that you charge on these cards, which typically carry a $25 to $50 annual fee, the sponsoring company rewards you with anything from free airline tickets, hotel stays, store discounts to cash. The more you charge, the more you get.

How to Avoid An Internal Revenue Service (IRS) Audit

The scariest letter any American can receive is one from the IRS suggesting that you come down to have a little chat about last year's return.

The first question asked by anyone receiving such a letter is "why me?" The answer is: only the IRS knows for sure, and they aren't talking. There are many reasons income tax returns are selected for audit, but the IRS keeps the details of the audit selection process secret — for obvious reasons.

Some audits are the result of an entirely random selection process, a kin to an audit lottery. Others are the result of the Periodic Taxpayer Compliance Measurement Program (TCMP) examinations which help determine areas of taxpayer abuse and help the IRS target areas ripe for audit success.

Certain geographical factors even factor into the audit equation — for example, you are more likely to be audited if you live west of the Mississippi River.

Stop Throwing Your Money Away!

According to a recent report, the IRS audits about 1 percent of all returns filed. But your odds of being audited may increase or decrease based on the level and type of income and deductions on your return. The following advice is not meant to be a comprehensive review, but being aware of these points could reduce your chances of being audited.

- Be accurate when listing business losses and home/office deductions. They are red flags.
- Be accurate when listing property (automobiles, computers, mobile telephones). This also invites scrutiny.
- Beware of the norms. The IRS uses them for comparison purposes.
- Loan application income should agree with tax return income.
- Use the appropriate depreciation schedules for all property and equipment.
- Do your math properly.
- Use the proper tax forms.
- Complete forms with all required data.
- Verify data on return.
- Attach federal income tax withholding forms.
- File returns on time.
- Properly sign and date your return.

Even if you do everything by the book, there's still a chance that you'll get audited. Relax, if you are properly prepared, there should be no reason to panic. The first thing you should do is decide if you or an expert, such as a certified public accountant (CPA) or an attorney, will participate in the audit. If you decide not to try it yourself, you should let the professionals make the contact and meet with the IRS.

How to Survive an Audit

Being prepared for the audit is *important*. the following is a list of suggestions that should help you survive an audit.

- Hold onto every receipt, invoice and voucher (keeping too much is better than too little).
- Respond to the contact letter in a timely manner.
- Be courteous and business like when dealing with the auditor.
- Be prepared to explain and support with adequate documentation every item of information on your return.
- Organize your records so that they are easy to find.
- Review the documentation supporting entertainment deductions to see that it indicates the required special information.
- Keep record of usage of listed property.
- Maintain records on an ongoing basis to avoid having to reconstruct data later.

General Tips
For Living an Audit-Free Existence

File a complete and accurate return. Seek assistance if you are uncertain about whether a particular form is required, how that form is to be completed, and whether an item should be included or how it should be calculated. Computer programs are now available, and there are many books that can help you in preparing your return. And yes, the IRS will answer your questions on the telephone. But it is not easy to get through to them, and their verbal answers may not be relied upon when you are audited. There are also state licensed tax return preparers, attorneys, and CPSs who specialize in preparing income tax returns and giving advice on complicated tax issues.

Finally, remember that you sign your return under a printed statement that refers to "Penalties of Perjury," so be careful out there.

Stewardship After Death

You may have heard about the family who was gathered in the attorney's office eagerly awaiting the reading of the last will and testament of a recently departed family member. It did not take the attorney long to read the very simple will, which merely stated, "being of sound mind, I have spent it all." I've seen bumper stickers in a similar vein which say, "we're spending our kids inheritance."

The assumption underlying both quotations is that a person can predict the time of death. If this were true, we could plan to have the last penny spent at the moment of death. Unfortunately, the most frequent comment you hear is that "Poor John didn't plan on dying so soon," even though Hebrews 9:27 clearly says, "it is appointed for man to die once, but after the judgment." Everyone will die; yet very few people plan on dying so soon.

Another reality is found in 1 Timothy 6:7, "for we brought nothing into this world, and it is certain we can carry nothing out." To paraphrase that verse: "You will never see a hearse pulling a U-Haul®." John D. Rockefeller's accountant was asked one time, "Can you tell he how much Rockefeller left behind?" The accountant replied, "Absolutely everything."

My perspective on estate planning is based on these realities: we will all die; we will take nothing with us; and we will probably die at a time other than when we would like. These realities create many practical planning problems.

Problems Associated with Death

The most significant problem with death is described in Romans 6:23, "for the wages of sin is death, but the gift of God is eternal life in Christ Jesus our Lord." He who dies without having accepted the gift of Jesus Christ as payment for his own sin is eternally separated from God.

Financial problems are non-existent in eternity. My prayer is that if any of you who read these words has never accepted the free gift of God's salvation, you would do so and make the most important estate planning step you can ever take. A simple prayer will lay the foundation for this estate: "Father, I acknowledge my separation from you, and based upon the death of the Lord Jesus Christ as payment for my sins, I accept the free gift of salvation. Thank you for saving me."

The second problem associated with death is really a set of problems related to finances. If you don't plan the distribution of your estate, the government will. Your spouse, relatives, or friends are not allowed to plan with distribution — only the owner of the assets can plan the distribution through a will. Very rarely does the government have the same objectives for your estate as you do. Additionally, if proper planning has not been done, the final expenses can siphon off up to 70 percent of an estate. These expenses are for probating the will, estate taxes, inheritance taxes, attorney's fee, accountant fees, and funeral expenses.

Another financial problem that occurs frequently because of poor planning is an estate without enough liquidity to meet the final expenses. Therefore, assets must be sold at depressed values just to generate the case needed for payoff expenses.

Another problem associated with death, or as the life insurance industry put it, "premature death," is that the survivors usually experience handling the details of an estate only once. Consequently, there are few experts and fewer yet who can be completely trusted to do things exactly as you would have them to. Therefore, these is a problem of making sure that the administration of the estate is handled as you would have it.

Being a good steward after death requires sound planning while you are alive in two areas: life insurance and estate planning.

Life Insurance Planning

The basic purpose of insurance is to transfer the risk that one is unwilling (or unable) to take to an entity willing to take the risk in return for compensation. In the case of life insurance, the objective is first to protect the family's income and net worth growth in the event of the bread winner's death. Second, it provides protection to maintain the estate in order that it might pass on to heirs, allowing the continuation of capital from one generation to the other.

Under the biblical system, when the father died, the oldest son assumed the bread winner's responsibility. If a man had no sons, then his brother undertook the care of the family through the laws God had established for widows and orphans (Deuteronomy 14:28, 290; James 2:27). Ideally, these caring functions today would be provided by the Body of Christ, the Church.

Unfortunately, they usually are not, so a vital part of family financial planning today includes continued provision through the use of life insurance.

You may say that purchasing insurance shows lack of trust in God to provide. Rather, this is the sound-mind principle being put to use. If you did not purchase insurance and you are married with children, upon your death, it is possible that your spouse would have to go on welfare (becoming dependent on the government). As a result, your family's spiritual and physical needs could go unmet. Insurance, on the other hand, would give your family the opportunity to continue to live in a proper environment.

How Much Insurance Do You Need?

You must first determine the insurance necessary to meet income goals and then adding to it, the amount needed for long-term liquidity needs such as major expenses and estate taxes in order to facilitate the transfer of your assets from one generation to the next, without tax erosion.

I use the simple formula that I learned about early in my insurance career called the "Dime Theory."

D – Death, burial expenses,
       other debts $ _____ .
I – Income Replacement
       (3 times annual salary) $ _____ .
M – Mortgage Payment $ _____ .
E – Education $ _____ .

While this may not be the most sophisticated formula, it is certainly one that will get you closer to where you should be with your life insurance program.

As a pastor, I can't tell you how many times I have seen families go to the funeral home knowing they can't even afford the cheapest funeral because the deceased failed to properly prepare.

What Type of Insurance Produce Do You Need?

Although insurance comes in hundreds of "wrappers," there are basically four different types of insurance policies. They are: term life (such as art and level premium five, ten, and twenty-year products). Traditional whole life, the Hybrid Product, (a combination of whole life and term), and universal life.

Annual Renewable Term

This product provides the maximum insurance coverage for the lowest initial premiums, with premiums increasing annually. The premium costs at older ages (age 60 to life expectancy) are prohibitive and make it difficult to maintain that type of policy until death. This product does not allow any flexibility in premium payments to meet changing circumstances. The obvious advantage of this type of coverage is the low initial cost, while the most obvious disadvantage is the high cost during the later years. In general, young families will provide the majority of their insurance needs with term insurance.

Traditional Whole Life

This product is more expensive initially than a term policy because of the level premiums and cash value building the policy requires. In a sense, the insurance owner overpays in the early years in order to underpay (or not pay) in later years. It's this aspect of a whole life policy that gives rise to the accumulation of cash value in the policy. This "forced savings" aspect of a whole life policy has been a controversial subject for many years. The primary disadvantage of a whole life policy is the high outlay of premiums required in the early years.

The Hybrid (Whole-Life/Term Combination)

This relatively new product has some characteristics of both whole life and term insurance. The premiums are typically lower than a traditional whole life product but higher than a term policy. There's a buildup of cash value on these policies, but at a lower rate than on the whole life policies. The percentage of whole life versus term insurance initially purchased will dictate the amount of the premium and the number of years you have to pay. Each year the policy will automatically buy paid up insurance to replace a portion of the term insurance. Over a period of time, the term is entirely replaced. In many cases, the owner can vary the level of term insurance initially and then add money to the contract with very little or no commissions taken out. Thereby improving the overall performance of this policy.

Universal Life

This relatively new type of insurance's primary advantage is the aspect of flexibility. It is flexible with regard to the death benefit as well as the premiums paid and the ability to withdraw cash from the policy.

Another possible advantage of a universal policy is that it can be more readily understood by the public. This contract is essentially a combination of an investment vehicle and term insurance. The insured makes premium payments to the contract which are credited with an interest rate on a monthly basis. Certain charges are taken out from the fund on a monthly basis. These include mortality costs and other administrative expenses.

A word of caution about universal life: the same feature that could be an advantage of this contract may become a disadvantage. The ability to vary the premium payments may put the insured in a position of having under funded the contract in later years and therefore seeing his coverage expire. This is particularly true when an agent or company has projected a high rate of return through the life of the policy, when in fact, the economic environment dictates that a lower interest rate is actually credited to his account during may of these year. Besides being able to vary the face amount of coverage and the premium payments, the policy also allows for withdrawals of cash value from the policy without actually borrowing on the funds.

In order for you to determine what kind of insurance plan you need, it's important for you to look at these insurance products from an overall prospective. This will mean asking the following questions: How much coverage do I need? How long do I need it? and How much coverage can I afford? Once you answer these questions, the appropriate product should become obvious.

Insurance is a wise cornerstone of a complete financial plan, and it's necessary for peace of mind in the family unit. Although the market place can be confusing, thinking through the issues raised in this chapter should help you arrive at a sound decision.

SOME QUESTIONS AND ANSWERS ABOUT INSURANCE

1. What if I can't afford the amount of insurance I need? *Get all you can with the money you have available.*

2. Does a non-working spouse need insurance? *Yes, if you can afford it. If not, be sure to insure the primary income earner.*

3. Do children need insurance? *If insurance funds are limited, provide coverage for the income earner(s) first. The purpose of insurance is provision. The children are not part of a family's provision.* There are four basic reasons for having insurance on a child:

- To provide guaranteed insurability. This is a major point used in seeking insurance for children. The idea implanted is that the child needs insurance in case he or she becomes disabled prior to becoming an adult and thus not qualifying for insurance.

- To give them direction into a quality company at an early age.

- For cash accumulation that can be used in purchasing other insurance policies at a later time.

- Low rates at an early start. Do not use insurance as a provision for education. Let your budget and your priorities be your guide.

Is Cash Value Insurance Always a Bad Buy?

No, just usually more expensive. The economic aspect of insurance savings need to be weighed carefully against other savings alternatives. Also, a long-term perspective may dictate a "permanent insurance product."

When is Cash Value Insurance a Good Investment?

When it disciplines the insured to save money which otherwise might not have been saved, or after a product may have been held more than five years.

Older policies may be a good investment even though the death benefit may be somewhat smaller than with new products.

When Do I Need Insurance?

When your reinvestment assets reach the point that the income derived from them, plus other income that will not change in the event of death, will meet the provision you are responsible for until that time. Insurance becomes an umbrella of protection to provide the needed resources in the event that you die before meeting your financial goals.

Retirement might be such a time. At retirement, income should be set. The source might be Social Security, pension plans, annuities, investments or a combination. If the spouse's needs are also met after the death of the provider, then there would not be a need for insurance to supply additional provisions. There would also have to be no anticipated estate tax or liquidity needs. At the other extreme, a young single person with no family or support responsibilities would have no need for insurance. An exception would be to have enough insurance so that burial costs or debt repayment would not present a burden to anyone.

Do Insurance Needs Change?

They certainly do. Because of this, you should perform a periodic review of insurance with respect to your overall financial position and provision requirements. For example, when a man marries, he's responsible to provide for his wife. This may precipitate an insurance need. When children come along, the need for insurance may increase because of the need to assure that they are provided for. Adequate capital is needed so the wife can still spend time training the posterity. As children gain independence, the provision needs may decrease.

Other factors which may prompt an insurance re-evaluation:
- A significant rise in inflation.
- Increased income or lifestyle costs.
- Heavy personal or business debt obligations.
- A change in estate liquidity needs.
- Long-term flexibility.

Is Insurance Scriptural?

There is no mention in Scripture of insurance. An assumption might be, therefore, that it is not unscriptural. The key is to have a balanced attitude toward it.

What About Mortgage Insurance?

Mortgage insurance is purchased for the exclusive purpose of paying off debt on the home in the event of the death of the homeowner. It's actually a decreasing term type of insurance because, as the debt decreases, the insurance company's liability is decreased. These policies are frequently more expensive than yearly renewable term products after the first several years.

Most mortgage insurance is very expensive when reduced to the dollar cost per $1000 of insurance base, especially if it's purchased through a mortgage company or bank. The alternative is to increase existing life insurance to provide this coverage, or to purchase a separate decreasing term life insurance policy for this purchase and cancel it when the mortgage is paid.

Do I Need Credit Life Insurance on My Loans?

Credit insurance is very expensive. It's not recommended for that reason alone. In many cases, however, it's required by the lender as a condition of the loan. In that case, your options are to find another lender, pay the price, save and pay cash, or forego the purchase.

BUDGET

Cash at the beginning of month	$ _____
Salaries/earned interest/ etc.	$ _____
TOTAL AVAILABLE FOR MONTH	$ _____

EXPENSES

Lunch expenses (school/work)	$ _____
Gas for auto	$ _____
Medical	$ _____
Recreation	$ _____
Clothing	$ _____
Donations (church, etc.)	$ _____
Household upkeep	$ _____
Auto upkeep	$ _____
Utilities (all)	$ _____
Insurances (all)	$ _____
Mortgage/Rent	$ _____
Groceries	$ _____
Miscellaneous	$ _____
Taxes	$ _____

SAVINGS:

Household Replacement	$ _____
Auto Replacement	$ _____
Emergency Fund	$ _____
TOTAL MONTHLY EXPENSES	$ _____
CASH BALANCE AT END OF MONTH	$ _____

What in the World Is Christian Stewardship?
TEST YOUR FINANCIAL FITNESS

Are you in good financial shape? Take this quiz to access your financial fitness. Circle your answers. If you answer yes to any of these statements, consult with a financial advisor about ways to manage your money better.

1. I generally am unable to keep track of where I spend money. yes / no
2. I do not have an emergency fund or I am not sure I have enough money available in case of an emergency. yes / no
3. I find it overwhelming to think about finances. The financial paperwork that crosses my desk each month is overwhelming. yes / no
4. I just experienced a major life change: new job, new spouse, new baby, etc. yes / no
5. I usually think about taxes around April 15. yes / no
6. I'm not sure the life, health and disability coverage I receive through my employer is enough for my family's needs. yes / no
7. We want to provide for our children's education. yes / no
8. I'm concerned I may run out of money during my retirement years. yes / no
9. My nest egg could work harder for me. yes / no
10. I want to leave an inheritance. yes / no

8

Tithing: A Personal Blessing Plan From Heaven

That which touches our wallets and purses taps a very sensitive nerve. When a person says, "it ain't the money but the principle of the thing," it's the money! Talk of giving makes us nervous, but the idea of tithing arouses feelings of hostility in some of us. Our immediate reaction is often to dismiss it as either "bringing in the law," or at least the classic example of a minister who has "quit preaching and gone to meddling."

My hope of convincing you is that: (1) you are a Christian; (2) you really want to please the Lord; and (3) you want to be governed by the Bible.

A Solution No One Talks About

Tithing is a solution no one talks about. If every professing Christian would tithe, every congregation would be free of financial worries and could begin to truly be, "the salt of the earth" (Matthew 5:13).

If every Christian would tithe, the Church would begin to make an impact on the world that would change it. The Church, instead, is paralyzed. Tithing Christians could make a big difference.

But because most Christians do not tithe, the churches remain in a generally discouraged state. Many churches struggle to pay their bills; electricity, water, heat, and pastor's salary. Perhaps a church will do something about redecorating its premises, or improving the building if there is any extra. In the mean time, money that might go to missions has to be kept at home. A handful of the faithful carry on most Christian work with precious little money.

The world is unimpressed with the church because the church has not commanded the world's attention and respect. When we do not support the work of God according to the biblical pattern, it should not surprise us that the world does not respect us. Why should they, when we don't respect God — or His way? We show how much we care according to how much we give.

Tithing is a solution to one's own spiritual problem. Part of the problem with your Christian growth has to do with fidelity in the stewardship of money. Sooner or later, every Christian faces the use of his money. What happens then? Either he will squarely and honestly face his Christian responsibility or he will draw back.

Jesus said: "He that is faithful in that which is least is faithful also in much" (Luke 16:10).

Becoming a tither provides a definite breakthrough for every Christian. It unlocks the door to the mind, heart and will. It releases, it emancipates, it frees. Becoming a tither is a milestone in every Christian's life. With some people tithing begins with conversion, but with others, it is a post-conversion commitment.

∽ **Tithing: A Personal Blessing Plan From Heaven** ∽

Tithing is as much a part of Christian gratitude and obedience as any commandment God ever gave.

The time will come when one actually will see the reward as tithing itself — not the blessing that emerges from doing. Tithing becomes its own reward when we learn thank God for the privilege of tithing.

Someone might say, "Surely one would be tithing with a wrong motive if he does it for a reward." I answer, "Who among us is so good and spiritual that he's impervious to any kind of promise of blessings? Who among us can do anything indefinitely without some kind of encouragement from God? Who can pray daily and faithfully for many days without there being some token of God's smiling?" All of us need encouragement. God knows this. "O taste and see that the Lord is good" (Psalm 34-8).

God is never too late, never too early; He is always just on time. Even though God would not have to promise a blessing if we obey, He always does. He deserves our obedience with or without any blessing. But, the truth is, God never demands obedience without a promise of blessing. "For He knoweth our frame; He remembereth that we are dust" (Psalm 103:14).

Obey Him, He will bless you. He loves to bless you. This is the way He is with His own. Our obedience moves His heart. He is touched by our gratitude. He cannot hide how He feels.

You cannot out-do the Lord. In tithing, you cannot out-give the Lord. He loves to bless those who honor him in this way. We must make a contract with the Lord, claiming the promise: "Them that honor me I will honor" (1 Samuel 2:30).

Tithing is not only a solution for the church at a financial level; but the same applies to the individual.

Remember, "He which soweth sparingly shall reap also sparingly; and which soweth bountifully shall reap also bountifully" (2 Corinthians 9:6).

The promises of Malachi 3:10 clearly point to a material return as one kind of blessing from the Lord. Obviously, some will prosper more than others, owing to gifts, place of responsibility or opportunity. But, at the bottom of it all is a promise for all believers that they will be honored (even at a material level) in such a way that, whether it be more or less than others, it is more than it would have been had they not been faithful in Christian stewardship. There are countless testimonies that could be brought forward of financial hardships, debt and distress, until tithing was begun. Not that such people became millionaires or drove Rolls-Royces, but that they lived without the terror or constant financial adversity.

WHY SOME CHRISTIANS DON'T TITHE

Three Basic Reasons

(1) Some Christians do not tithe because they simply have not been taught to tithe. It must start in the pulpit. The pastor must be a tither. He must teach it to his people. Christian parents must teach their children to tithe.

(2) Some Christians do not tithe because they do not understand of the place of God's Law in the Bible.

The moment one raises verses such as "the tithe is the Lord's" (Leviticus 27:30), or "Will a man rob God?" (Malachi 3:8), someone else is usually around who says, "But that's the Old Testament. We are not under the law but under grace."

But is not the very word "tithe" an Old Testament term? Yes. Nearly everything we as Christians believe originated in the Old Testament. Words like "faith," "atonement," "redemption," "righteousness," "sin," etc., have their origin in the Old Testament. But not in the Law. The big mistake we so often make is that we say — if it is in the Old Testament it must be under the Law. This is wrong. "The law is not of faith," said Paul (Galatians 3:12). Men like Abel, Noah, Abraham, Isaac, Jacob, and Joseph did what they did by faith (Hebrews 11:23-32), and this took place after the Law came. The writer of the epistle to the Hebrews would have us follow all these men.

> (3) Some Christians do not tithe because they refuse to do so. Some are convinced, others don't want to be convinced; but at bottom is a refusal to part with what we regard as "ours."

Someone has said "If you don't tithe, God will get it anyway." Not that God will get it for His work, but He most certainly has a way of keeping us from enjoying the entire 100 percent.

WHY EVERY CHRISTIAN SHOULD TITHE

There is ultimately only one reason why every Christian should be a tither: *because it is biblical.*

All of us need encouragement with regard to giving. None of us, by nature, is a tither. We will look for every possible loophole by which we can justify our not tithing. Our Lord will not let us do that.

- You should tithe because of what it will do for the work of God on earth. Look at Malachi 3:10 – "Bring ye all the tithes into the storehouse, that there may be meat in mine house." The same

God who claims to own "the cattle upon a thousand hills" (Psalm 50:10), and whom the nations are but as a "drop of a bucket" (Isaiah 40:15), equally claims His dependence upon His people to return to Him what is rightfully His — namely, the tithe.

"The tithe is the Lord's." As a consequence, the prophet Malachi regards the withholding of any tithe as robbing God.

God owns everything but will accept nothing unless freely given to Him. In a word: God depends on His people to tithe. There is nothing more sad than an underpaid minister. In most cases, were every member to tithe, the minister would not only receive his "double honor" (1 Timothy 5:17) but the church would always have money to pay for its material needs.

- You should tithe because of what it will do for God in heaven. What on earth, you may ask, can tithing do for God? Answer: Much. How so? Because He loves us so much. God has invested Himself in us. God gave us His Son, and those who dignify His Son's work on the cross have eternal life.

- We should tithe because of what tithing does for us. God blesses obedience. He waits to bless us. He wants to bless us far more than we want the blessing. But He waits to see whether we take Him seriously.

What tithing does for us, then, is realized at two levels: the natural and the spiritual. The spiritual is by far the most important, for the very blessing that comes from heaven is essentially spiritual. It is God telling us He is pleased with us.

Tithing is one way to find great spiritual release. When one enters the life of faithful tithing, there is a sweet release to be experienced that cannot be fully explained to another person. This release by itself is enough to fully convince one how serious God is about tithing. The peace and joy are so wonderful that a frequent reaction is a kind of sorrow that one had not been doing it sooner.

God has a way of blessing us materially that just happens to coincide with our having become tithers. The 90 percent that we keep to ourselves after the tithe is given to the Lord has a way of equaling the 100 percent before the tithe. Sometimes the percent goes far, far beyond what that 100 percent would have purchased. How can this be? Frankly, I do not know. But I believe it.

THE ORIGIN OF TITHING

Tithing is not a twentieth-century innovation, although there is some reason to believe that it has spread more widely in the last hundred years than in previous generations of the Christian church.

Tithing, however, was revived more as a practice than a doctrine in recent times, and the definitive statement on this subject has yet to be written.

It is generally believed that Abram was the first tither.

The first time the word tithe appears in the Bible is in Genesis 14:20: "He giveth him tithes of all. He (Abraham) gave him (Melchizedek) *tithes* of all" (a tenth of everything).

There is no indication that Abraham was told to tithe by Melchizedek himself. The Mosaic Law, which later made tithing a legal obligation, actually came over 400 years later. Therefore, Abraham was not keeping any prescribed command or law of God.

A straightforward reading of Abraham's giving to Melchizedek tithes suggests that this was done gratefully, voluntarily but also systematically.

The tithe comes from the "increase" or income. Abraham did what he did voluntarily. There was no Mosaic Law in force, then neither is there any indication that Melchizedek came along and "assessed" Abraham to the tune of 10 percent. Melchizedek was not God's IRS agent. The government assesses — as does the Mosaic Law. But God puts those who have been touched by the gospel on their honor.

Abraham was not promised a blessing for giving the tenth. He already had been blessed!

Abraham gave not only voluntarily but also systematically. He gave one tenth of all. Abraham was careful to give a "tenth of everything." That is our example. Let us follow his gratitude that we may be cheerful givers (2 Corinthians 9:7). Abraham paid tithes to Melchizedek. Melchizedek was a figure of Christ.

When the Mosaic Law made tithing legal and binding on Israel, it was the Levitical priesthood to whom tithes were to be paid (Numbers 18:21).

Therefore, Abraham's giving to Melchizedek prefigured the New Testament pattern, that those who preach the gospel "should receive their living from the gospel" (1 Corinthians 9:14). The tithes of all paid by all would enable every minister of the gospel to live at this standard.

Tithes, therefore, should be solely and exclusively for the work of the gospel. Tithes should not be given to "charity," or any noble work.

When a Christian gives his tithes, or any part of them, to non-church organizations — no matter how valuable or useful to society they may be — that Christian robs the church and therefore God.

The tithe, therefore should go directly and only into the storehouse — the ecclesiastical service of God. Charitable organizations should be sustained by either non-Christians or Christians who have first given all their tithes to the church and then to that organization.

I think we must therefore say that Abraham did what he did voluntarily and yet he had no choice. He did not have to tithe and yet he did have to tithe. He volunteered, but he could not do anything else. Martin Luther had a choice but uttered that famous statement, "Here I stand. I can do no other. God help me. Amen."

This seems to be the way tithing originated. Nothing has really changed since.

The Gospel and the Law

A common objection to tithing is that it is bringing in the law. Some say: "We are not under the law, but under grace" (Romans 6:14); therefore, tithing is "out" insofar as the Christian is concerned.

Freedom from the Law of Moses is precisely what prepares one for the happy yoke of Christ's Lordship. Freedom "from" is also freedom "for."

"Take my yoke upon you", said Jesus, "and ye shall find rest unto your souls. For my yoke is easy, and my burden is light" (Matthew 11:29-30).

Under the new covenant — the gospel of Christ — we have the freedom of self-discipline precisely because of our faith, not obedience, counts for righteousness (Romans 4:3-5). Tithing is not a carry-over from the Mosaic Law. It is a carryover from Abraham.

God does not enforce tithing today. But, to the person who is under Christ's Law there will be given — sooner or later — the light of tithing God's way. When we are given the light of tithing, we show at that moment whether or not we submit to the yoke of Jesus Christ. "His commandments are not burdensome" (1 John 5:3). Indeed, they pave the way for blessings beyond all we could have dreamed.

THE BLESSING OF TITHING

There was a man,
Some called him mad;
The more he gave
The more he had.

— John Bunyan —

The Bible is full of promises of blessing on the apparent condition of obedience.

The promises of blessing in the Bible are often set in the language of accommodation. God stoops to our level to encourage us. He reaches us where we are. "He knoweth our frame; He remembereth that we are dust" (Psalm 103:14).

We, therefore, would do ourselves an immense favor if we checked out our motives for tithing from the beginning. The danger is that we will be motivated to tithe for the wrong reason. A godly concern must lie behind our tithing or we could set ourselves up for a very deep disappointment.

There are some biblical texts concerning giving and being blessed that bear looking into. Perhaps the most outstanding is Malachi 3:10. Some may object to this verse because it comes within the parenthetical period of the Law. However, most of the Old Testament does. Does that mean we ignore it? We would have to omit the Psalms as well.

Malachi 3:10 reads: "Bring the whole tithe into the storehouse, that there may be food in my house. Test me in this, says the Lord Almighty, and see if I will not throw open the floodgates of heaven and pour out so much blessing that you will not have room enough for it."

This command and promise is set in the context of a severe warning to the children of Israel. "Will a man rob God?" Yet ye have robbed me. But ye say, wherein have we robbed thee? In tithes and offerings.

The reason withholding tithes may be said to be robbing God ought to be fairly obvious to the reader by now. The tithe...is the Lord's (Leviticus 27:30). What Abraham had given to Melchizedek turns out to be nothing more than what was actually God's all along! The tithe is already the Lord's. He claims the 10 percent of the increase on income from the start. It is not a question whether or not God should have it; it is His — already. He says so. But, the remarkable thing is, He puts us on our honor to turn it over to Him. The same principles lies behind Paul's words: "For ye are bought with a price" (1 Corinthians 6:20).

In other words, the Corinthian Christians were told by Paul that their bodies were already God's — not merely by creation but by redemption, the price being the blood of God's own Son. Thus, the Corinthians were not their own. Yet Paul said to them: "Therefore, glorify God in your body, and in your spirits, which are God's (1 Corinthians 6:20). If they did not glorify God in this manner, they asked two things: (1) the loss of their reward in heaven (1 Corinthians 3:15); and (2) their very lives.

What in the World Is Christian Stewardship?

Tithing, although obeying a commandment at a different level, is no different in God's sight. As the body is the Lord's, so the tithe is the Lord's. To abuse the body is to abuse the temple of the Holy Spirit, so also is the withholding of God's tithe to rob Him of what is His own. He puts us on our honor to obey Him. Not to do so results in our spiritual impoverishment, perhaps even our peril.

For Malachi continued: "Ye are cursed with a curse; for ye have robbed me, even this whole nation." It would seem from this that the people of God in Malachi's day found other uses for their money. Perhaps they couldn't "afford" to tithe. Perhaps they thought the tithe really didn't matter all that much. "But, says Malachi, look around you, haven't you noticed? You are cursed with a curse. You are in trouble as a nation. The reason is that you have literally robbed God!"

Malachi's message is most fitting and relevant (but no less unpleasant) today. Every nation under the sun seems to be in financial difficulty. An unbalanced budget, rising inflation, low cash flow, high unemployment, and bewilderment, and on and on. The root of the problem is the failure of God's people to tithe.

If every member of the Christian church would give 10 percent of his annual income — even if this should be the maximum, one can safely predict that "there will be meat" in God's house.

This, then, is the chief motive for tithing is not the blessing that we will get from obedience. The chief motive is that we are jealous for God's work, that we want it to thrive and prosper, that there be no hindrance whatever owing to the lack of funds. We give because we care. We give because we know God has used men to advance his work. Tithing is God's way.

What is sadder than a church that is run down? What is sadder than a minister of the gospel who can hardly pay his bills? What is sadder than the general feeling of financial oppression, in so far as, the church is concerned? All this can only be true because the people of God have robbed God of what is His. It is not only disgraceful, it is sad. All of us must hang our heads in shame when we consider the state of the church at the present time in most places. Tithing is one way of rectifying this. There are other ways, of course, but tithing is one way in the meantime.

Why should you be a tither? That there may be meat in God's house. Why should you be a tither? Because you care about the work of the Lord.

If no one else in your congregation is a tither, you must begin tithing now because you care about your own relationship with God. It is He who sees what you do that matters. There is no better reason for tithing than that.

At this stage Malachi makes one of the most extraordinary claims in all Holy Writ. What follows is, to me, one of the most remarkable lines in the Bible. Here follows the only place in the Bible we are told to prove God. "Prove me now herewith, saith the Lord of hosts." This is extraordinary. There is no other place in the word of God that suggests proving God. The Bible, in fact, makes no attempt to prove God. It only begins: "In the beginning God" (Genesis 1:1).

Do you want to prove that God is alive and well? Do you want to prove that God still does things? Honor Him with your substance and you will see Him in a manner that will exceed your greatest expectation.

In singular kindness and tenderness, God stooped to motivate us. He condescended and put His own reputation on the line. This is why there are innumerable testimonies as to the blessings people have received from tithing. God honors obedience. This is not an absolute promise. It is based on obedience.

What is it that God suggests will follow our tithing? That He will open the windows of heaven. Not only will you receive spiritual blessings but material blessings will be yours, also.

Once a person comes upon the light of tithing he must go one or two ways: forward or backward. If you draw back from tithing, once you have been exposed to it, I predict that the light in the soul will become dim, if not dark indeed. But, should you walk in this light, the primary result will be spiritual release from within. You will feel not only "good" inside but will notice a new glow in living the Christian life, a renewed appreciation for studying God's Word. And, you'll be easier to live with! I promise it.

Malachi encourages us to believe that if we truly give God what is His by honoring Him with our substance, He will, in turn, do things for us that can be visibly seen and felt at a material or natural level. "I will rebuke the devourer for your sakes" (Malachi 3:11). That is God's promise.

The Bible is full of similar promises. Honor the Lord with thy substance, and with the first-fruits of all thine increase! So shall thy barns be filled with plenty, and thy presses shall burst out with new wine (Proverbs 3:9,10).

Give and it will be given to you. A good measure, pressed down, shaken together and running over, will be poured into your lap. For with the measure you use, it will be measured to you (Luke 6:83).

One man gives freely, yet gains even more; another withholds unduly, but comes to poverty (Proverb 11:24).

> *There was a man,*
> *Some called him mad;*
> *The more he gave*
> *The more he had.*
>
> – John Bunyan –

A generous man will prosper; he who refreshes others will, himself, be refreshed (Proverb 11:25).

Remember this: whoever sows sparingly will also reap sparingly, and whoever sows generously shall reap also generously (2 Corinthians 9:6).

Tithing is, in fact a Christian duty. It comes under our Lord's summation in Luke 17:10; "... So likewise ye, when ye shall have done all those things which are commanded you, say, we are unprofitable servants; we have done that which is our duty to do." (We are unworthy servants; we have only done our duty). And yet, God delights in showing that He is pleased with us. It is as though He cannot keep from concealing His own pleasure with us. So what does He do? He shows it. He has shown it for so long and so often and to so many that no one knows who said it first: "You cannot out give the Lord."

DO YOU TITHE?

Do you tithe? The logical answer to that question would be yes or no, depending upon whether you give ten percent of your income to the Lord. But, do you tithe? In the Old Testament, the Jews gave a tithe of everything they possessed, so do you really tithe?

Were ten percent of the miles on your car put there service the Lord? There are 161 hours in every week. Do you spend 16 hours every week doing something for Jesus? Are 10 percent of your telephone calls made for Jesus? Are 10 percent of the programs you watch religious in nature? Can you honestly say that 10 percent of your reading time is spent reading the Bible or some other Christian literature? Now certainly every Christian should give 10 percent of their income to the Lord, but God gives us much more than money, therefore, we owe Him more than money.

I like what Paul said about giving in 2 Corinthians 8:5: "And this they did, not as we hoped, but first gave their own selves to the Lord, and unto us by the will of God." God is not merely interested in your money, He is interested in you. He wants to be first in every area of your life. That is what the Lordship of Jesus is all about; letting Jesus be Lord of everything.

There are three kinds of givers — the flint, the sponge, and the honeycomb. To get anything out of the flint, you must hammer it and then you get only chips and sparks. To get water out of the sponge, you must must squeeze it. The honeycomb, however, just overflows with its own sweetness.

SCRIPTURE STUDIES ON TITHING

The following Scripture studies can enrich your life as a Christian steward. Read the suggested Scripture references carefully. Reflect on the meaning and make personal application.

(1) The Old Testament Teaches Three Tithes

Numbers 18:21-24 (for the Levites), Deuteronomy 12:5-9 (for worship celebrations), and Deuteronomy 14:28, 29 (for charity)

∽ Tithing: A Personal Blessing Plan From Heaven ∽

NUMBERS 18:21-14 –
For the Levites

And behold I have given the children of Levi all the *tenth* in Israel for an inheritance, for their service which they serve, even the service of the Tabernacle of congregation. Neither must the children of Israel henceforth come nigh the Tabernacle of the congregation lest they bear sin and die. But the Levites shall do the service of the Tabernacle of the congregation, and they shall bear their iniquity; it shall be a statue forever throughout your generations, that among the children of Israel they have no inheritance. But the *tithes* of the children of Israel, which they offer as a heave offering unto the Lord, I have given to the Levites to inherit; therefore I have said unto them, among the children of Israel they shall have no inheritance. (vv. 21-14)

DEUTERONOMY 12:5-9
FOR WORSHIP CELEBRATIONS

But unto the place which the Lord your God shall choose out of all your tribes to put His name there, even unto His habitation shall ye seek, and thither thou shalt come. And thither ye shall bring your burnt offerings, and your sacrifices, and your *tithes*, and heave offerings of your hand, and your vows, and your freewill offerings, and the firstlings of your herds and of your flocks. And there ye shall rejoice in all that ye put your hand unto, ye and your household, wherein the Lord thy God hath blessed thee. Ye shall not do after all the things that we do here this day, every man whatsoever is right in his own eyes. For ye are not as yet come to the rest and to the inheritance which the Lord your God giveth. (vv. 5-9)

∽ What in the World Is Christian Stewardship? ∽
DEUTERONOMY 14:28, 29
For Charity

At the end of three years thou shalt bring forth all the *tithe* of thine increase the same year, and shalt lay it up within thy gates. And the Levite (because he hath no part nor inheritance with thee), and the stranger, and the fatherless, and the widow, which are within thy gates, shall come, and shall eat and be satisfied: that the Lord thy God may bless thee in all the works of thin hand which thou doest. (vv. 28-29)

1) The Tithe Belongs to God – Leviticus 27:30-32

And all the *tithe* of the land, whether of the seed of the land, or of the fruit of the tree, is the Lord's; it is holy unto the Lord. And if a man will at all redeem ought of his *tithes*, he shall add thereto the fifth part thereof. And concerning the *tithe* of the herd, or of the flock, even of whatsoever passeth under the rod, the *tenth* shall be holy unto the Lord. (vv. 30-32)

(2) Tithes Are to be Taken to the Place that God Designates – Deuteronomy 12:1-28; 14:22-27

Thou shalt truly *tithe* all the increase of thy see, that the field bringeth forth year by year. And thou shalt eat before the Lord thy God, in the place which He shall choose to place His name there, the *tithe* of thy corn, of thy wine, and of thine oil, and the firstlings of thy herds and of thy flocks; that thou mayest learn to fear the Lord thy God always. And if the way be too long for thee, so that thou art not able to carry it, or if the place be too far from thee, which the Lord thy God shall choose to set His name there, when the Lord thy God hath blessed thee. The thou shalt turn it into money, and bind up the money in thine hand, and shalt go unto the place which the Lord thy God shall choose. And thou shalt bestow that money for whatsoever thy soul lusteth after for oxen, or for sheep, or for wine, or for strong drink, or for whatsoever thy soul desireth; and thou shalt eat there before the Lord thy God, and thou shalt rejoice, thou and thine household. And the Levite that is within thy gates; thou shalt not forsake him; for he hath no part nor inheritance with thee. (vv. 22-27)

(3) God Promises to Bless Those Who Tithe — Malachi 3:10-12

Bring all the *tithes* into the storehouse, that there may be meat in mine house, and prove me now herewith, saith the Lord of Hosts, if I will not open the windows of heaven, and pour you out; a blessing, that there shall not be room enough to receive it. And I will rebuke the devourer of your sakes, and he shall not destroy the fruits of your ground; neither shall your vine cast her fruit before the time in the field, saith the Lord of Hosts. And all the nations shall call you blessed: for ye shall be a delightsome land, saith the Lord of Hosts. (vv. 10-12)

(4) Tithing Involves More Than Money – Deuteronomy 14:22, 23

Thou shalt truly *tithe* all the increase of thy seed, that the field bringeth forth year by year. And thou shall eat before the Lord thy God, in the place which he shall choose to place His name there, the *tithe* of thy corn, of thy wine, and of thine oil, and the firstlings of thy herds and of thy flocks; that thou mayest learn to fear the Lord thy God always. (vv. 22-23)

(5) Jesus Commends Tithing While Emphasizing the Importance of Positive, Spiritual Attitudes – Matthew 23:23

Woe unto you, scribes, and Pharisees, hypocrites! For ye pay *tithe* of mint and anise and cummin, and have omitted the weightier matters of the law, judgement, mercy and faith; these ought ye to have done, and not to leave the other undone (v. 23).

(6) Tithing Is Not the Limit for Christian Givers — John 3:16; Mark 12:41-44

For God so loved the world that He gave His only begotten Son, that whosoever believeth in Him should not perish, but have everlasting life (3:16).

Mark 12:41-44

And Jesus sat over against the treasury, and beheld how the people cast money into the treasury; and many that were rich cast in much. And there came a certain poor widow, and she threw in two mites, which make a farthing. And He called unto Him His disciples, and saith unto them, Verily I say unto you, That this widow poor widow hath cast...into the treasury. "For all they did cast in of their abundance; but she of her want did cast in all that she had, even all her living.(vv. 41-44)

(7) Tithing Can be Misused Through Spiritual Pride – Luke 18:10-14

Two men went up into the Temple to pray; the one a Pharisee and the other a Publican. The Pharisee stood and prayed thus with himself, God I thank thee, that I am not as other men are, extortioners, unjust, adulterers, or even as this publican. I fast twice a week, I give *tithes* of all I possess. And the Publican, standing afar off would not lift up so much as his eyes unto heaven, but smote upon his breast, saying God be merciful to me a sinner. I tell you, this man went down to his house justified rather than the other; for every one that exalteth himself shall be abased; and he that humbleth himself shall be exalted. (vv. 10-14)

SCRIPTURE REFERENCES ON TITHING AND GIVING

Malachi 3:10 — Bring ye all the tithes into the storehouse, that there may be meat in mine house, and prove me now herewith, saith the Lord of hosts, if I will not open you the windows of heaven, and pour out a blessing that there shall not be room enough to receive it.

Matthew 23:23-24 — Woe unto you, scribes and pharisees, hypocrites! for ye pay *tithe* of mint and anise, and cummin, and have omitted the weightier matters of the law, judgement, mercy, and faith: these ought ye to have done, and not to leave the other undone. Ye blind guides, which strain at a gnat, and swallow a camel.

Luke 18:12 — I fast twice in the week, I give *tithes* of all that I possess.

Genesis 14:20 — And blessed be the most high God, which hath delivered thine enemies into thy hand. And he gave him *tithes* of all.

Genesis 28:22 — And this stone which I have set for a pillar, shall be God's house: And of all that thou shalt give me I will surely give the *tenth* unto thee.

Leviticus 27:30 — And all the *tithe* of the land, whether of the seed of the land, or of the fruit of the tree, is the Lord's: It is holy unto the Lord.

2 Chronicles 31:5 — And as soon as the commandment came abroad, the children of Israel brought in abundance the firstfruits of corn, wine, and oil, and honey, and of all the increase of the field; and the tithe of all things brought they in abundantly.

Nehemiah 10:30 — And the priest the son of Aaron shall be with the Levites, when the Levites shall bring up the tithe of the tithes unto the house of our God, to the chambers into the treasure house.

Nehemiah 13:12 — Then brought all Judah the tithe of the corn and the new wine and the oil unto the treasuries.

Nehemiah 12:44 — And at that time were some appointed over the chambers for their treasures, for the offerings, for the firstfruits, and for the tithes, to gather into them out of the fields of the cities the portion of the law for the priests and Levites.

QUESTIONS ABOUT TITHING

1) Should we tithe the "gross" or the "net"?

The Lord's tithe is ten percent of our gross salary or income. We must remember that whatever is deducted from our gross pay is for our own good. Sooner or later somehow we get it back. Remember God puts us on our honor to give to Him what is His.

2) Why should I tithe when my actual tithe is so small?

You should do it because it is right. The amount is utterly irrelevant. God sees the heart. That makes all the difference. Not the actual amount. In any case, the tithe is still the Lord's.

3) Is the storehouse "always the church?"

In my understanding of scripture – yes (1 Corinthians 9:14, Deuteronomy 25:4, 1 Timothy 5:1). The tithe is to be entrusted to the church so that the church may make the proper decisions as to its use.

4) Can my tithe be sent to any other ministry that upholds God's work, like a missionary or Bible society, a Christian organization or even a TV ministry?

One cannot bypass the local church in any way and be true to God's Word. It is the church that ought to support a missionary society or any other valid ministry doing the work of the Lord. We must not rob the storehouse.

5) What if one cannot afford to tithe?

The answer is, we cannot afford not to tithe. Who can afford to rob God?

6) What if I am the only tither in my church?

What one does in this case is between that person and God. God sees what is happening. In the end, that is all that really matters. You are the one who is enriched. You do not tithe for public recognition.

7) Isn't tithing a hardship on the poor?

No, it is not. The tithing plan is God's plan, and it is the most fair and reasonable arrangement in the world. The poor person has to pay as much for food as the rich person. Gas costs the poor person as much as it costs the rich person. But, if a man has a smaller income, he has a smaller tithe. Yet, he should still give the tithe. Tithing gives dignity to every person.

8) Should I tithe if I am heavily in debt?

Yes. How much money do you think God would get if He had to wait for all of us to get out of debt? A person who is heavily in debt should consider getting professional advice on debt consolidation.

9) Should a person keep personal records of his or her own giving?

Yes. It is a good business practice. It is one way of assuring yourself that at the end of the year that your tithe actually equaled or exceeded ten percent of your annual income.

10) Should children tithe?

Yes, if they have income. The best time to learn is while they are young.

9

Stewardship Messages

*WHERE IS YOUR TREASURE?

*A CERTAIN RICH MAN

*WILL A MAN ROB GOD?

*CHRISTIANS ARE STEWARDS OF GOD

• • • • • • • • •

WHERE IS YOUR TREASURE?
Luke 12:34

Introduction: "Treasure: Accumulated wealth, money, gold. Any person or thing considered valuable: to value greatly."

While the writer Luke affirms Christ divinity, the real emphasis of his book is to show His humanity. Jesus, the Son of God, is also the Son of man. As a doctor, Luke was a man of science, and as a Greek, he was a man of detail. In addition Luke was a close friend and traveling compassion of Paul, so he could interview the other disciples, had access to other historical accounts, and was eye witness to the birth and growth of the early church. His gospel and book of Acts are reliable, historical documents.

Luke's story begins with angels appearing to Zacharias and then Mary, telling them of the birth of their sons. From Zacharias and Elizabeth would come John the Baptist who would prepare the way for Christ. And Mary would conceive by the Holy Spirit and bear Jesus, the Son of God.

Luke gives us a glimpse of Jesus at age 12 — discussing theology with the teachers of the law at the Temple. The next event occurs eighteen years later, when we read of John the Baptist preaching in the wilderness. Jesus came to John to be baptized before beginning His public ministry. At this point, Luke traces Jesus' genealogy on His earthly father Joseph's side, through David and Abraham back to Adam, underscoring His identity as the Son of Man.

Beginning at verse 22, Jesus warns about worry. As a matter of fact, He commands us not to worry. But how can we avoid it? Only our faith can free the anxiety that is caused by greed and covetousness. It is good to work and plan responsibility; it is bad to dwell on all the ways our planning could go wrong. Worry is pointless because it cannot fill any of our needs. Worry is foolish because the creation of the universe loves us and knows what we need.

Where is your treasure? In other words, where is your concern? What's important to you? What place do you give God in your life?

You should make the kingdom of God your primary concern. You should make Jesus Lord of your life. He must control every area — work, play, your plans, your relationships. If we put Him first, He knows and will provide what it is that we need.

We must understand that God wants to use what we have; money, time, talent, gifts, to be a blessing to others. When we use what we have to help others we invest in our heavenly bank account. We lay up treasure in heaven.

You must understand that you cannot separate what you do from what you believe. What you treasure reveals your true priorities. So I challenge you — Where is your treasure? Most men live for the here and now, but we must live for later and forever.

Closing: Where is your treasure? I've come to understand that if a man's treasure is in earthly things — he spends all his time accumulating earthly things. If his treasure is in his career – he spends all of his time working – no time for family, God. If a man's treasure is in power, he spends his time in his quest for power. But if his treasure is in heaven – he is like the man in Psalm 1: "His delight is in the law of the Lord; and in his law doth he meditate day and night. And he shall be like a tree planted by the rivers of waters, that bringeth forth fruit in his season; his leaf also shall not wither, and whatsoever he doeth shall prosper" (vv. 2-3).

When your treasure is in the right place, you can identify with David: "The Lord is my shepherd, I shall not want" (Psalm 23:1)

He provisions David, who later said, "I've been young, now I'm old – I've never seen righteous forsaken or his seed begging bread" (Psalm 37:25).

Where is your treasure? – Are you doing it your way or are you trusting God?

> "My hope is built on nothing less,
> than Jesus's blood and righteousness;
> I dare not trust the sweetest frame,
> but wholly lean on Jesus' name.
> On Christ the solid rock I stand.
> All other ground is sinking sand
> All other ground is sinking sand."

Where is your treasure? Keep trusting in God When you don't know what to do, just wait on Him.

• • • • • • • • •

A Certain Rich Man
Luke 16:14;19-31

Introduction: The pharisees considered wealth a proof of righteousness. Jesus startled them with this story in which a diseased beggar is rewarded and a rich man is punished. The rich man did not go to hell because of his wealth, but because he was selfish with it. He did not feed Lazarus, take him in, or care for his health.

He was hard-headed in spite of his great blessings. The amount of money we have is not so important as the way we use it. Rich people can be generous or stingy – and so can poor people.

The rich man – ate well, dressed well, enjoyed the best of everything that life could offer. Yes, he was set for life – but what about eternity?

Lazarus was the poor beggar, who simply requested the rich man's garbage from his table. Lazarus was not only poor, but he was also sick. The Bible says he had sores on his body. To make matters worse the dogs came and licked his sores. What a very stark contrast between two men. One may ask how could life be so good to one and unfair to the other. How could one man have so much and the other have so little?

Yes this parable draws a stark contrast between the rich man and the poor man. The key to understanding it is to know who Jesus was telling it to: the Pharisees whom Luke describes as lovers of money (v-14). Like the rich man, they were set for life – but not for eternity. They displayed an image of righteousness but were actually hypocrites (v-15). They were careful to preserve the Mosaic tradition, but they violated the spirit of the Mosaic Law. Worst of all they rejected Jesus as the Christ.

So what happens when we are set for life but not for eternity?

The beggar died and was carried away by the angels to Abraham's bosom. The rich man also died and was buried. Not much fanfare for a man who had so much going for him while he lived. He had everything in life, but nothing in death. Set for life but not for eternity.

He lifts his eyes in hell – Lazarus goes to Abraham's bosom – a place of rest and peace. The rich man looks up and sees Lazarus afar off and begs Abraham to let him stick his finger in cool water to cool his tongue. My, how things have changed! Abraham reminds him that while he lived he had everything and Lazarus had nothing. But things have changed.

Then he begs for his five brothers, but Abraham says they have Moses and the prophets.

You might be asking yourself just what is God trying to tell me in this story? He was not saying that all poor people will go to heaven nor was he saying that all rich people will go to hell. He was warning those who live as though this life is all that matters.

The insensitive rich man received his "good things" during his lifetime. He was like the man described in Psalm 17:14, who has his portion in this life, but has no portion in the life to come, or like those in Psalm 73, the wicked who have it all. They live above the everyday problems. They have more wealth than they will ever need, yet they belittle those who live hand to mouth. With all of their status and power, they strut through life not even caring for God. But in eternity, the tables tend to turn. The rich man is poor and the poor man is rich.

We must learn – whatever we have – God has given it to us so that we can be a blessing to someone else. We must refuse to be set for this life and totally unprepared for eternity. What about it? Do you have your business fixed?

• • • • • • • • •

WILL A MAN ROB GOD?
Malachi 3:8-13

Introduction: The book of Malachi forms a bridge between the Old Testament and the New Testament. The purpose of this the last book of the Old Testament is written to confront the people with their sins and to restore their relationship with God. It is written to the Jews in Jerusalem and God's people everywhere.

He tells us God loves – perfecting and completely. His love is a love of action — giving, guiding, and guarding. He is altogether faithful, true to His promises to His chosen people. But consistently they spurn their loving God, breaking the covenant, following other Gods, and living for themselves. So the relationship is shattered.

But the breach is not irreparable; all hope is not lost. God can heal and mend and reweave the fabric. Forgiveness is available, and that is grace. This is the message of Malachi, God's prophet in Jerusalem.

Malachi concludes with a promise of the coming of another "prophet like Elijah" who will offer God's forgiveness to all people through repentance and faith.

The people sacrificed to God wrongly in three different ways:
(1) Expedience - being as cheap as possible.
(2) Neglect - not caring how they offered the sacrifice.
(3) Outright disobedience - doing it their own way and not as God had commanded. Their giving reflected their attitude toward God.

I. The Sinful Priest

God tells the people of his deeply rooted love for them. He charged the priest with failing to honor Him and failing to be good spiritual examples to the people. The Temple was rebuilt in 516 B.C., and worship was being conducted there, but the priest did not worship God properly.

The worship of God had lost its vitality and had become more of a business for the priests than heartfelt adoration. God accused Israel of dishonoring Him by offering polluted sacrifices.

Our lives should be living sacrifices to God. If we give God only our leftover time, money, and energy, we repeat the same sin as these worshippers who didn't want to bring anything valuable to God. What we give God reflects our attitude toward Him.

From a practical standpoint it made sense for the Jews to keep the best animals for themselves and to sacrifice the unwanted ones. But these sacrifices were to God, and God deserves the very best.

II. The Sinful People

(1) The priest had allowed influential and favored people to break the Law. They were so dependent on these people for support that they could not afford to confront them when they did wrong.

(2) The people were being unfaithful in their homes. They were living as if God didn't exist. They acted like they could do anything and not be punished.

(3) They became complacent which led to blatant sin, such as marriage to those who worshiped idols.

(4) The people were complaining about their adverse circumstances when they had only themselves to blame.

III. The Coming of the Lord

But it also tells about Malachi urging the people to stop holding back their tithes, to stop keeping from God what He deserved. The tithing system began during the time of Moses (Leviticus 27:30-34; Deuteronomy 14:22). The Levites received some of the tithe because they could not possess land of their own (Numbers 18:20, 21).

The people ignored God's command to give a tithe of their income to His Temple.

Closing: So the question becomes obvious–"Will a man rob God?" We rob banks–we rob each other–but do we have the audacity to rob God?

God asks and God answers, "Yes, we rob Him–in tithes and offerings."

We rob Him when we fail to offer ourselves a living sacrifice. How could we rob God, when God gives us so much. He gave us Jesus. He gave His life. His life gave us another chance!

Stop robbing God. Let Him open heaven's windows for you. He'll bless you if you let Him. He'll take care of you if you let Him.

• • • • • • • • •

CHRISTIANS ARE STEWARDS OF GOD
Psalm 24:1-2

Text: "The earth is the Lord's and the fullness thereof; the world and they that dwell therein" (Psalm 24:1).

Dominion: "To rule over." – God made the human race a steward to rule over His creation (Genesis 1:26).

Steward/Treasurer — one who manages what has been entrusted to him/her as the owner requires.

Two Kinds of Stewards

(1) Faithful Steward: One who obeys the master in managing what has been entrusted in their care. "Moreover it is required in stewards, that a man be found faithful (1 Corinthians 4:2).

(2) Unfaithful Steward: One who refuses to obey the Master's commands in managing what has been entrusted to him.

"If therefore, ye have not been faithful in the unrighteous mammon (money), who will commit to your trust the true riches?" (Luke 16:11) "And if ye have not been faithful in that which is another man's who shall give you that which is your own?" (Luke 16:12)

The Faithful Steward and the Lord's Tithe

(1) He/she returns the Lord's tithe because he/she acknowledges God as owner of everything (Psalm 24:1; Malachi 3:10).

(2) Tithing glorifies God (1 Corinthians 10:31; Psalm 29:1, 2; Romans 4:20).

(3) Tithing demonstrates a profound and absolute trust in God Almighty (Proverbs 3:5, 6).

(4) Tithing demonstrates that the believer looks to God for supply of all need (Philippians 4:19).

(5) Tithing demonstrates a profound love for the Lord (John 14:15).

(6) Tithing acknowledges that Jesus Christ is our Lord (Luke 6:46).

(7) Tithing demonstrates that we have submitted our selfish will to God's holy, divine and everlasting will (Ephesians 6:6).

(8) Tithing demonstrates we do not want to do things our way (Proverb 14:12).

(9) Tithing honors God (Proverb 3:9).

The Faithful Steward and Giving from the 90 percent

(1) The steward is required to give bountifully (2 Corinthians 9:6).

(2) The steward is required to give cheerfully (2 Corinthians 9:7).

(3) The steward is to give consistently (1 Corinthians 6:2).

(4) The steward is to give as God has prospered him (1 Corinthians 16:2).

(5) The steward is to give because Jesus said so (Acts 20:35; Luke 6:38).

God's Promises to the Faithful Steward

(1) God will overflow the faithful steward with abundant blessings (Malachi 3:10).

(2) God will provide for all your needs (Philippians 4:19).

(3) God will fix it so you'll always have something to give and food to eat. (2 Corinthians 9:10; Psalm 37:25).

(4) God will give the faithful steward power to get wealth (Deuteronomy 8:18).

Abraham: The First Steward to Return the Tithe

(1) Abraham believed God (Romans 4:20).

(2) Abraham knew that whatever God promised, He would do (Romans 4:21).

Believe God through faith (Hebrews 11:6) Doubt God through unbelief (John 20:25).

There was a man
They called him mad
The more he gave
The more he had

Appendix

Resource Material for Stewardship Use

LEND A HAND

I am only one But still I am one I cannot do everything, But still I can do something; And because I cannot do everything, I will not refuse to do the something that I can do.

– Edward Everett Hall
1822—1909

CHRISTIAN PARADOX

It is in loving—not in being loved the heart is blest; It is in giving—not in seeking gifts, we find our guest. If thou art hungry, lacking heavenly food—give hope and cheer. If thou art sad and wouldst be comforted stay sorrow's team. Whatever be thy longing and thy need, That do thou give so shall thy soul be fed, and thou indeed, shalt truly live.

– Author Unknown

Simple Litany for an Offering Service

LEADER: Why should we give?

RESPONSE: Remember the words of the Lord Jesus, how He said, "It's more blessed to give than to receive" (Acts 20:35).

LEADER: How should we give?

RESPONSE: "Every man as he is able, according to the blessing the Lord has given you" (Deuteronomy 16:17).

LEADER: To whom should we give?

RESPONSE: "He who loves God, loveth his brother, also" (1 John 4:21)

References Used

Tithing—A Call to Serious, Biblical Giving, R.T. Kendall. Grand Rapids, Michigan: Lamplighter Books; Zondervan Publishing House, 1982.

What the Bible Says About Stewardship, A.R. Fagan.; Nashville, Tennessee: Convention Press, 1976.

All the Parables of the Bible, Herbert Lockyear. Grand Rapids, Michigan: Zondervan Publishing House, 1963

How to Live on Twenty-Four Hours a Day, Arnold Bennett. New York: Ayer Company Publishers, 1976.

"The Solid Rock" written by Edward Mote.

Notes

Notes

Printed in the United States
140322LV00001B/45/A